UNDERSTANDING ACCOUNTING

UNDERSTANDING ACCOUNTING

Stanley H. Stern
Adjunct Professor, Management
Antioch University
Los Angeles, CA

ARCO PUBLISHING, INC.
New York

Published by Arco Publishing, Inc.
215 Park Avenue South, New York, N.Y. 10003

Library of Congress Cataloging in Publication Data

Stern, Stanley H.
  Understanding accounting.

  Includes index.
  1. Accounting.   I. Title.
HF5635.S837   1983   657   82-18434
ISBN 0-668-05726-2 (Reference text edition)
ISBN 0-668-05673-8 (Paper edition)

Printed in the United States of America

10 9 8 7 6 5 4 3 2 1

To my father:
All my love and respect

Contents

Introduction—
"Financial Data Doesn't Bite"

The principles and practices of business and tax accounting, although necessary, practical, and straightforward, have for generations caused the owners of small businesses, non-accounting managers, and millions of taxpayers undue trauma, sweaty palms, and queasy stomachs. According to a well-known and widely used university-level accounting textbook, accounting is "the art of analyzing and recording financial transactions and certain business-related economic events in a manner that facilitates classifying and summarizing the information, and reporting and interpreting the results." The accounting (a/c) establishment, by deviously comingling a "foreign" language (a/c jargon) with mathematics, has been able to keep a financial stranglehold over the small business scene since Biblical times. Then the moneychangers were thrown out of the temple for keeping two sets of books. Today, the mere mention of a *debit* or a *credit*—let alone the thought of analyzing, recording, classifying and, finally, interpreting financial data that might eventually be scrutinized by the I.R.S.—is enough to panic the average citizen and bring tears of joy to the average accountant.

The profession of accountancy is divided into two categories: one that serves the general public; the other that serves business enterprises. *Public accountants*, who become *certified public accountants (CPAs)* after passing a licensing exam, serve as independent practitioners. Their primary function is to audit and review the work of *management* or *in-house accountants*. Without

governmental and public auditors, businesses would be free to compile financial data and to interpret it as they wish. The use of "creative accounting" would thus take on expanded importance. Management accountants, also known as *private accountants*, are employed by, and perform the accounting for, a certain business or individual.

A knowledge of accounting is useful to people who operate businesses or make management decisions. Such knowledge is also useful to people whose activities bring them into contact with business and financial matters, for example, people employed by business and governmental agencies. These people often need to use accounting data in their work or private lives. The ability to read and to interpret an annual report can make any decision to buy a stock or a bond less frantic.

As an experienced teacher of basic and intermediate accounting courses to hundreds of anxious and apprehensive* adults, I came to realize the urgent and immediate need for a book that would help remove the veil of mystery that shrouds accounting. The useful skills and principles necessary to perform essential accounting and recordkeeping operations can now be available to anyone who is willing to throw off the dread and walk with his or her head erect into the world of financial data, without having to go through migraines, insomnia, and a course at Berlitz.

* Possibly insurance salesmen, TV repairmen, plumbers, and mechanics make adults more apprehensive.

Now, with your fear under control and your supply of pencils* sharpened, you are ready to begin. Remember—neatness is mandatory and three-piece suits optional. Also, a calculator is a suitable tool with which to avoid the embarrassment of trying to recall how to perform long-lost mathematical operations, such as adding and subtracting. Learning the skills and acquiring the knowledge that will save you time, money, and embarrassment at cocktail parties will also, around the 15th of April, allow you too to say: "H & R Block, eat your heart out!"

* Don't get too cocky too soon and try to use a pen. Build your confidence one chapter at a time.

UNDERSTANDING ACCOUNTING

CHAPTER 1

The Language of Accounting—
"You Don't Have to Be
Bilingual"

The purpose of business accounting is to provide useful information about the financial operation and condition of a business firm to the individuals, the organizations, and the governmental agencies who have the need and the right to be so informed. The interested parties include the following:

1. The firm's owners, both present and future
2. Management personnel, a/c and non-a/c staff
3. Creditors and suppliers of goods and services
4. Governmental agencies—local, state, and federal

Although the preceding explanation relates to virtually every form of business enterprise known to man, the average person has to be a linguist to translate this essential information into his or her native tongue. Therefore, competitors, clients, suppliers, trade associations, labor unions, and governmental agencies all have to hire accountants to interpret the data compiled by other accountants. What this does is perpetuate the need for more accountants and, thereby, confuse the rest of us.

So, for the same reason that doctors say *anhypnosis* when they mean *insomnia*, and lawyers write *rusticum jus* instead of simply saying *justice*, accountants have their own special language. Having its own jargon enables members of the accounting fraternity to feel equal to other natural and social scientists who are able to charge exorbitant fees for translating their mumbo jumbo into English, French, German, Japanese, or Swahili. When an accountant speaks of a debit, he or she means the information that is on the left side. Wouldn't it be simpler to say *left* instead of *debit*, or *right* instead of *credit*? Of course! But any reasonably intelligent three-year-old understands what *left* and *right* mean. Therefore, it behooves accountants to confuse us in order to prove they know more than young children.

As a believer in the use of clear and concise language, I will attempt to translate fifty primary and elemental accounting terms so that you can make sense of financial statements, year-end reports, bank statements, ledgers, journals, and bills from your accountant. This lexicon (that's vocabulary for you non-writers) of accounting terminology will hopefully remove the first layer of fear from all you non-accountants who think of accountants as the enemy.

ACCOUNTING TERMINOLOGY

ACCOUNTING	The recording and reporting of all business transactions ,for use in making future business decisions.
ACCOUNTING CYCLE	Source documents, journal, ledger, trial balance, adjustments (accruals), adjusted trial balance, income statement, balance sheet, closing entries, and post-closing trial balance.
ACCOUNTING EQUATION	Assets = Liabilities + Owner's equity.
ACCOUNTING PERIOD	The length of time for which an income statement is customarily prepared.
ACCOUNTS PAYABLE	An amount owed to a creditor (liability), generally on an open account.
ACCOUNTS RECEIVABLE	A claim against a debtor (asset) from sales of goods or services.
ACCRUAL	The recognition that the recording of a revenue or expense transaction (i.e., accounts receivable or accounts payable) might occur in one a/c period, while actual payment is made in another a/c period.
ALLOWANCE	A deduction given by the creditor for damage, delay, shortage, or imperfection, which is subtracted from the amount owed.
ALLOWANCE FOR DOUBTFUL ACCOUNTS	A business expense showing the accounts receivable that were not paid.
ASSET	Anything of monetary (cash) value owned by a business (e.g., furniture, equipment).
AUDIT	Any inspection by a third person (i.e., CPA) of accounting records involving analysis, testing, proof, and confirmation.
BALANCE SHEET	A statement showing the status of all assets, liabilities, and owner's equity on a specific date.
BOARD OF DIRECTORS	A group chosen by the stockholders to operate a corporation.
BOOKKEEPING	The recording of financial data from source documents to journals and ledgers.
CAPITAL	The owner's investment in a business; **not** synonymous with *cash*; it can include cash, equipment, furniture, etc.
CASH	Money (currency and coins), money orders, bank deposits, and bank credit card balances; the first asset listed on a balance sheet.
CASH DISCOUNT	The amount (%) that a supplier will deduct from the total price for prompt payment.
CHART OF ACCOUNTS	A numerical list of all assets, liabilities, capital, revenue, and expense accounts.
CORPORATION	A legal form of ownership, based on a charter, where the owners' participation in profits and loss depends upon how many shares they own.
COST OF GOODS SOLD	The price paid for the merchandise a business sells.
CREDIT	To record information on the *right* side of an account.
DEBIT	To record information on the *left* side of an account.
DEPRECIATION	The monetary loss in service, capacity, or utility from a fixed asset (e.g., automobile); a type of business expense.
DIVIDEND	Cash paid to stockholders from a corporation's retained earnings (net income); payment is authorized by the Board of Directors.
EXPENSE	A cost of operating a business (e.g., telephone, salaries); also called **OVERHEAD**.
GENERAL JOURNAL	Book of original bookkeeping entries, where data from source documents is first recorded.
GENERAL LEDGER	A book of accounts whose information comes from the General Journal.

GROSS MARGIN (GROSS PROFIT)	Total sales minus the cost of goods sold; also called **MARKUP**.
HISTORICAL COST	The original cost of an asset; actual cost.
INCOME STATEMENT	A statement providing information about revenue and expenses over a specific period of time.
INVENTORY	An asset representing the sum total of finished goods, materials, supplies, and merchandise on hand.
LIABILITY	An obligation of a business to pay a debt (i.e., accounts payable, notes payable) to a creditor.
LIMITED PARTNER	The liability is limited *only* to the amount of the partner's investment.
LIQUIDITY	Conversion of accounts receivable and other assets into cash.
NOTE	An unconditional written promise to pay a certain sum of money (i.e., I.O.U.).
OWNER'S EQUITY	Capital + Income − Expenses; the net worth of a business.
PARTNERSHIP	Two or more people who combine resources in a business based upon provisions of a partnership agreement.
PAYROLL	A record showing the wages and salaries earned by employees, and the various deductions for withholding taxes, insurance, disabilities, etc.
PETTY CASH (FUND)	A small amount of cash on hand available for minor disbursements, where payment by check is impractical.
POSTING	The process of recording information from a journal to the General Ledger.
PREPAID EXPENSES	Current assets (i.e., supplies) that become expenses as they are used.
PROVING	Verifying the accuracy of an amount by comparing the totals in two places (i.e., debits = credits).
PURCHASES	Any properties (assets), goods, or services acquired; when used (i.e., supplies), it becomes a business expense.
REVENUE (SALES, FEES)	Any source of income for a business.
SINGLE PROPRIETORSHIP	A business with one owner who has unlimited liability for all debts.
SOURCE DOCUMENTS	Business papers that supply the initial information about a business transaction (i.e., sales slip).
STOCKHOLDERS (SHAREHOLDERS)	The owners of the capital stock (shares) of a corporation.
TRADE DISCOUNT	The amount (%) that a supplier will deduct from the total price for prompt payment.
TRANSACTION	Any business activity involving an exchange of money values (e.g., purchasing assets).
TRIAL BALANCE	A list of all accounts proving the ledger; debits must equal credits.

CHAPTER 2

The Accounting Equation— "No Higher Mathematics, Just Common Sense"

> **ASSETS (A) = LIABILITIES (L) + OWNER'S EQUITY (O.E., net worth)**

Etch this *accounting equation* forever in your mind and everything that follows will make sense to you. Trust me! The relationship between these three basic accounting elements is the same from the beginning of a business to the end of its existence and every day in between. It is *never* out of balance. If you can recall some high school algebra, you know that it is possible to move numbers from one side of the equal (=) sign without changing the value of the equation. Therefore:

1. Assets = Liabilities + Owner's equity
2. Liabilities = Assets – Owner's equity
3. Owner's equity = Assets – Liabilities

When two elements are known, it is easy to calculate the third. For example, Mr. Stern has business assets of $50,000 and business debts (liabilities) of $38,300. To find the amount of Mr. Stern's equity, you just express the facts in equation form as follows:

a. Owner's equity = Assets – Liabilities
b. O.E. = $50,000 – $38,300
c. O.E. = $11,700

In order to increase his equity in the business, Mr. Stern must increase his assets without increasing his liabilities, or decrease his liabilities without decreasing his assets. So, in order to increase his owner's equity and his assets (and I have great faith that he will), Mr. Stern can either invest more capital in the business or operate the business at a profit, which is definitely the way to go. For example, if one year later Mr. Stern's owner's equity amounted to $18,000 and his liabilities amounted to $33,600, the status of his business would be:

a. Assets = Liabilities + Owner's equity
b. A = $33,600 + $18,000
c. A = $51,600

If Mr. Stern had not increased or decreased his investment, the difference in owner's equity of $6,300 would have been due to profit (net income).

TYPES OF ACCOUNTS

To insure that the accounting equation remains in balance, *all* business transactions and events that affect the three elements—assets, liabilities, and owner's equity—must be recorded by the bookkeeper. Everything that has a monetary effect on a business does affect the accounting equation and the five types of accounts involved.

ASSETS	Cash and property of value owned* by a business. Properties such as merchandise (inventory and supplies), furniture, fixtures, equipment, machinery, cars, trucks, land, buildings and receivables. Accounts receivable are unwritten promises and notes receivable are written promises by a firm's customers to pay at a later date for goods or services. Each and every asset should have a separate ledger account.
LIABILITIES	An obligation, either written or unwritten, of a business to pay a debt. All liabilities including accounts payable, notes payable, and the inevitable and unavoidable local, state, and federal taxes *must* include the word *payable*. An account payable is an unwritten promise to pay a debt in the future. Each and every liability should have a separate ledger account.
CAPITAL	It represents the owner's investment (share) in the business. It is not synonymous with cash because capital can also include other property (car, land, typewriter, etc.) that the owner invests in his business.
REVENUE	Any source of income for a business. Revenue includes sales of goods, charges (fees) for services rendered, interest received from savings accounts, investments, and notes receivable. Each and every source of revenue should have a separate ledger account.
EXPENSES	Any cost of operating a business. It is also known as **OVERHEAD**. Expenses include salaries, utilities, interest, taxes, insurance, and supplies. Each and every expense should have a separate ledger account.

HOW TRANSACTIONS CAN AFFECT THE ACCOUNTING EQUATION

All transactions in a business enterprise involve the exchange of values, which are always expressed in terms of money. The buying and selling of property and services, whether for cash or on credit, are standard transactions. Each transaction affects one or more of the three basic accounting elements. For example, the purchase of fixtures for cash represents the increase of one asset (fixtures) and an equal decrease in another asset (cash). The total amount of assets remains the same, so the accounting equation is unaffected and remains in balance. The effect of any transaction on the accounting equation is accomplished by addition or subtraction only. If you're using a calculator, I'm referring to the + or − buttons.

* It is owned even if it has not been paid for. The amount owed is a liability.

Examples

TRANSACTION:

Mr. Stern (I just love that name) opens a consulting business and invests $25,000 in cash. This transaction illustrates an increase in an asset balanced by an increase in owner's equity.

A	=	L	+	O.E.
Cash				S. Stern, Capital
$25,000	=	$0	+	$25,000

TRANSACTION:

Mr. Stern purchases office furniture for $1,500 on 60 days credit. This transaction illustrates an increase in an asset offset by an increase in a liability.

A		=	L	+	O.E.
Cash +	Office Furniture		Accounts Payable		S. Stern, Capital
$25,000	$1,500		$1,500		$25,000

A	=	L	+	O.E.
$26,500		$1,500		$25,000

TRANSACTION:

Mr. Stern pays $1,000 for a copying machine. This transaction illustrates an increase in an asset offset by a decrease in another asset.

A			=	L	+	O.E.
Cash	+ Office Furniture	+ Office Equipment		Accounts Payable		S. Stern, Capital
$25,000	$1,500	$1,000		$1,500		$25,000
− 1,000						
$24,000	$1,500	$1,000		$1,500		$25,000

A	=	L	+	O.E.
$26,500		$1,500		$25,000

TRANSACTION:

Mr. Stern pays $1,000 on account to the company from which he purchased the office furniture. This transaction illustrates a decrease in an asset offset by a decrease in a liability.

A			=	L	+	O.E.
Cash	+ Office Furniture	+ Office Equipment		Accounts Payable		S. Stern, Capital
$24,000	$1,500	$1,000		$1,500		$25,000
− 1,000				− 1,000		
$23,000	$1,500	$1,000		$ 500		$25,000

A	=	L	+	O.E.
$25,500		$500		$25,000

TRANSACTION:

Mr. Stern receives $1,250 from a client as a consulting fee (revenue). This transaction illustrates an increase in an asset offset by an increase in owner's equity.

A			=	L	+	O.E.	
Cash	+ Office Furniture	+ Office Equipment		Accounts Payable		S. Stern, Capital	+ Revenue
$23,000	$1,500	$1,000		$500		$25,000	$1,250
+ 1,250							
$24,250	$1,500	$1,000		$500		$25,000	$1,250

A	=	L	+	O.E.
$26,750		$500		$26,250

TRANSACTION:

Mr. Stern pays a phone bill (expense) of $50. This transaction illustrates a decrease in an asset offset by a decrease in owner's equity.

A			=	L	+	O.E.		
Cash	+ Office Furniture	+ Office Equipment		Accounts Payable		S. Stern, Capital	+ Revenue	− Expense
$24,250	$1,500	$1,000		$500		$25,000	$1,250	$50
− 50								
$24,200	$1,500	$1,000		$500		$25,000	$1,250	$50

A	=	L	+	O.E.
$26,700		$500		$26,200

Before you proceed to Chapter 3, make sure you understand the principle of the accounting equation. Every business transaction or activity may affect the totals of the element, but *the left side of the equation (assets) will always equal the right side (liabilities + owner's equity)*. The equation is *always* in balance; everything that follows is based on that fundamental rule. (*Note:* Exercises and problems for practice for Chapter 2 will be found combined with those for Chapter 3, and have been placed at the end of Chapter 3.)

CHAPTER 3

Financial Statements—
"If You Know the Questions,
They Have All the Answers"

A set of accounting records is maintained so that it can be used to fulfill a variety of financial and managerial needs. Foremost is its use as *source documents* for the preparation of various reports, referred to as *financial statements*. The two most important of these are the *income statement* and the *balance sheet*.

Because the income statement and the balance sheet summarize the accounting data from all ledgers and journals, and are extensions of the accounting equation, I have found that it is extremely helpful to study these financial statements prior to discussing bookkeeping. In this case, the cart definitely belongs before the horse.

THE INCOME STATEMENT

Sometimes called a *profit-and-loss statement* or *operating statement*, the income statement represents the *revenue* and the *operating expenses* for a specific period of time (i.e., month, quarter, year). If your total revenue is higher than your total expenses, the difference is *net income*. But if your total expenses exceed your total revenue then, I'm sad to say, you have a *net loss*. Since over fifty percent of all new businesses do not last more than one year, net losses are rather common.

A simple income statement relating to the service business of Mr. S. Stern (when you write a book, you can use your own name) for the month ending September 30, 19____ is shown in Illustration 3.1. It has two basic sections—the revenue received and the expenses incurred during September.

The form used in the income statement is standard, so anyone can easily read and interpret it. A double line under a number indicates it is a final total (i.e., net income).

If Mr. Stern owned a business that sold a product, the income statement would contain an additional section—*cost of goods sold* (see Illustration 3.2). Cost of goods sold is subtracted from revenue to give you the difference, *gross profit* or *gross margin*. Although not listed as an expense, it is a cost of operating the business and more properly should be called expense of goods sold. For example, the price that a clothing store pays the manufacturer of the clothing is the cost of goods (clothing) sold. An example of an income statement for a clothing (product) business for the month ending September 30, 19____ is shown in Illustration 3.2.

ILLUSTRATION 3.1

S. STERN, CONSULTING *(name of firm)*
Income Statement *(type of report)*
For Month Ending September 30, 19___ *(accounting period)*

Revenue:
Fees (sales of services) $10,000

Expenses:
Salaries expense	$1,125
Rent expense	800
Insurance expense	125
Postage expense	50
Supplies expense	200
Miscellaneous expense	90

Total expenses 2,390
Net income for month .... $ 7,610

ILLUSTRATION 3.2

STERN'S GLAD RAGS
Income Statement
For Month Ending September 30, 19___

Revenue:
Sales $50,000
Cost of goods sold:
Beginning inventory, September 1, 19___ $10,000
+ Purchases during month 40,000

Goods available for sale $50,000
Less: Ending inventory, September 30, 19___ 10,000

Cost of goods sold 40,000
Gross margin from sales $10,000

Expenses:
Salaries expense	$ 1,125
Rent expense	800
Insurance expense	125
Postage expense	50
Supplies expense	200
Miscellaneous expense	90

Total expenses 2,390
Net income for month .... $ 7,610

The reason the income statement is prepared prior to the balance sheet is that the net income or net loss will be added to, or subtracted from, the capital in the owner's equity section of the balance sheet.

THE BALANCE SHEET

Sometimes called a *position statement*, the balance sheet shows the *net worth* of a business on a specific date. As an expanded version of the accounting equation, the balance sheet shows the assets, the liabilities, and the owner's equity.

The assets section includes:

1. **Current assets**—Those which are cash or can be converted to cash in 90 days. Cash, petty cash, accounts receivable, merchandise inventory, and any prepaid expenses (i.e., supplies and insurance).
2. **Fixed assets**—Store equipment, fixtures, machinery, office equipment, furniture, land, buildings, cars, and trucks.

The liabilities section includes:

1. **Current liabilities**—Those debts that will become due (payable) within one year. Accounts payable, notes payable, and con-

tracts payable generally become due in 60 or 90 days.
2. **Fixed liabilities**—Long-term contracts payable, mortgage payable, and long-term notes payable that will become due in longer than one year.

The owner's equity section includes:

1. **The owner's capital**—His investment.
2. **The owner's drawing**—The amount withdrawn from the business for the owner's *personal* use (i.e., vacations, clothing, dance lessons, roller skates).
3. **Net profit or net loss**—The amount that comes from the income statement for that period.

An example of a balance sheet for a clothing company owned by—you guessed it—Mr. S. Stern as of September 30, 19____ is shown in Illustration 3.3.

ILLUSTRATION 3.3

STERN'S GLAD RAGS
Balance Sheet
As of September 30, 19____

ASSETS			LIABILITIES		
Current assets:			*Current liabilities:*		
Cash	$18,000		Accounts payable	$ 6,100	
Accounts receivable	9,000		Notes payable	1,700	
Inventory	10,000		Total current liabilities		$ 7,800
Prepaid expenses	2,200				
Total current assets		$39,200	*Fixed liabilities:*		
			Contracts payable	$ 3,500	
Fixed assets:			Notes payable	1,500	
Store equipment	$12,500		Total fixed liabilities		5,000
Office equipment	2,700		Total liabilities		$12,800
Furniture	1,700				
Automobile	6,500				
Total fixed assets		23,400	**OWNER'S EQUITY**		
Total assets		$62,600			
			S. Stern, capital	$42,190	
			Net income	7,610	
			Total owner's equity		49,800
			Total liabilities and owner's equity		$62,600

As with the accounting equation, assets = liabilities + owner's equity in the balance sheet. *Just think of the line down the middle as an equal sign (=).*

The balance sheet above shows the *net worth* of a *single proprietorship* (one owner). If Mr. Stern had a partner or partners, or if he incorporated his store, the only change in the financial state- ments would occur in the owner's equity section of the balance sheet. A single proprietorship, a *partnership*, and a *corporation* are the three legal forms of ownership. The operation of the firm and the accounting functions remain exactly the same for all three forms of ownership. Illustra- tions 3.4 and 3.5 show the changes in the propri- etory worth of a company.

ILLUSTRATION 3.4

STERN & HUGHES GLAD RAGS
Balance Sheet
As of September 30, 19____

	Total liabilities $12,800
	PARTNERS' EQUITIES
	S. Stern, capital $21,095
	S. Stern, net income .. 3,805
	H. Hughes, capital ... 21,095
	H. Hughes, net income 3,805
	Total partners' equities 49,800
Total assets $62,600	**Total liabilities and partners' equities** . $62,600

ILLUSTRATION 3.5

GLAD RAGS, INC.
Balance Sheet
As of September 30, 19____

	Total liabilities $12,800
	STOCKHOLDERS' EQUITY
	Capital stock outstanding $42,190
	Retained earnings ... 7,610
	Total stockholders' equity 49,800
Total assets $62,600	**Total liabilities and stockholders' equity** $62,600

In a corporate balance sheet, *capital stock outstanding* equals the value of all the shares owned by the stockholders (one or more). *Retained earnings* is the net income of a corporation from which any dividends are declared.

An auditor or a prospective buyer can learn a great deal about the financial viability of a firm by analyzing its financial statements. Among the principles that can be determined from financial statements are:

1. **Ratio analysis**—Comparing the relationship between two figures in a balance sheet.

   a. **Current ratio**—A prime measure of liquidity.

   $$\text{Current ratio} = \frac{\text{Current assets}}{\text{Current liabilities}}$$

   This ratio should be at least 2:1 ($\frac{2}{1}$) for a company to be considered soundly financed.

   b. **Quick ratio**—The "acid test" of liquidity.

   $$\text{Quick ratio} = \frac{\text{Cash plus Receivables}}{\text{Current liabilities}}$$

   This ratio should be at least 1:1 ($\frac{1}{1}$). In other words, cash plus receivables should equal or exceed current liabilities. This will definitely insure that a company can pay its current debts. And believe me, creditors frown on not getting paid.

   c. **Working capital**—The difference between current assets and current liabilities.

   $$\text{Working capital} = \text{Current assets} - \text{Current liabilities}$$

   Working capital provides the ability to meet current operating expenses.

   d. **Proprietorship ratio**—The relationship between the owner's investment (capital) and the total assets.

   $$\text{Proprietorship ratio} = \frac{\text{Capital}}{\text{Total assets}}$$

   A 1:2 ($\frac{1}{2}$) or 50% ratio will generally insure soundness in financial structures. Less than 50% means an owner borrowed more than he or she invested, and it will extremely limit his or her ability to borrow in the future.

2. **Income statement analysis**

   a. $$\text{Amount of markup} = \text{sales} - \text{cost of goods sold}$$

   $$\text{Percent of markup} = \frac{\text{Gross margin}}{\text{Total sales}}$$

   The percentage should generally equal 1:2 ($\frac{1}{2}$) or 50% for most retail and wholesale firms.

   b. **Inventory**—Is the inventory on hand adequate for sales volume?

   c. **Operating expenses**—Are operating expenses (overhead) in line with the most efficient firms of this type? You can compare annual reports of firms to get this information.

As the title of this chapter indicates, the answers to the questions about a firm's financial stability can be found in the income statement and the balance sheet, *if* you know where and how to look. The data in these statements comes from the recordkeeping (bookkeeping sounds so . . . menial) functions of accounting, which will be discussed in Chapter 4.

It is now time to restore the cart to its proper place, behind the horse.

Carry on!

EXERCISES AND PROBLEMS
FOR CHAPTERS 2-3

The Accounting Equation and Financial Statements

Exercises

1 . The March Company has total assets of $264,000 and the owners' equity is $77,000. What is the amount of the company's liabilities?

2. The items included in the balance sheet of ABC Company as of June 30, 19____ are listed below out of proper sequence. Arrange the items in balance sheet form and compute the capital for John Smith.

Land $30,000	Building $70,000
Notes payable $75,000	Equipment $3,400
J. Smith, capital ?	Accounts payable $14,600
Accounts receivable $18,900	Cash $12,100

3. Make four columns on a sheet of paper and head them as follows:

Trans-action	Total Assets	Total Liabilities	Total Owner's Equity

You are to identify each of the following transactions by letter. Then, next to each transaction, indicate its effect on the total assets, liabilities, and owner's equity by placing a plus sign (+) for an increase, a minus sign (−) for a decrease, and the letters (NC) for no change.

a. Purchased a typewriter on credit.
b. Owner invested cash into the business.
c. Purchased office equipment for cash.
d. Received payment for an accounts receivable.
e. Owner withdrew cash for personal reasons.
f. Paid a liability.
g. Returned some office furniture bought on credit.

As an example, transaction a. would be shown as follows:

Trans-action	Total Assets	Total Liabilities	Total Owner's Equity
a.	+	+	NC

Problems

1. ABC Company and XYZ Company are in the same line of business. Since both were recently organized, it may be assumed that the recorded costs for assets are close to current market values. The balance sheets for the two companies as of July 31, 19____ are on page 14.

REQUIRED

A. Assume that you are a banker and that each company has applied to you for a 90-day loan of $12,000. Which would you consider to be the more favorable prospect?
B. Assume that you are an investor considering the purchase of one or both of the companies. The owners of ABC and XYZ have each indicated to you that they would consider selling their respective businesses. In either transaction, you would have to assume the existing liabilities. For which business would you be willing to pay the higher price? Explain your answer fully. (It is recognized

that for either decision, additional information would be useful, but you are to reach your decisions on the basis of the information available.)

ABC COMPANY
Balance Sheet
As of July 31, 19____

ASSETS		LIABILITIES	
Cash	$ 4,800	Notes payable	
Accounts receivable	9,600	(due in 60 days) ... $62,400	
Land	36,000	Accounts payable ... 43,200	
Building	60,000		
Office equipment	12,000	Total liabilities $105,600	
Total assets	$122,400		
		OWNER'S EQUITY	
		Ed Adams, capital	16,800
		Total liabilities and owner's equity	$122,400

XYZ COMPANY
Balance Sheet
As of July 31, 19____

ASSETS		LIABILITIES	
Cash	$24,000	Notes payable	
Accounts receivable	48,000	(due in 60 days) $14,400	
Land	7,200	Accounts payable ... 9,600	
Building	12,000		
Office equipment	1,200	Total liabilities $24,000	
Total assets	$92,400		
		OWNER'S EQUITY	
		Tom Baker, capital	68,400
		Total liabilities and owner's equity	$92,400

2.

T. SMITH AGENCY
Trial Balance
March 31, 19____

Cash	101	$ 6,372.10	
Stationery and supplies	112	1,238.05	
Office furniture	121	4,052.40	
Notes payable	201		$ 1,980.00
Accounts payable	212		1,415.24
T. Smith, capital	301		7,737.12
T. Smith, drawing	312	1,386.88	
Professional fees	401		3,711.84
Rent expense	501	330.00	

Telephone expense	502	47.52
Salary expense	503	616.00
Travelling expense	504	696.34
Stationery and supplies expense	505	40.55
Miscellaneous expense	506	64.36
Totals		$14,844.20 $14,844.20

REQUIRED

A. Prepare an income statement for the T. Smith Agency showing the results of the first month of operations, March.

B. Prepare a balance sheet for the T. Smith Agency, in account form, showing the financial condition of the agency as of March 31, 19____. Use a sheet of two-column statement paper for the income statement. Two sheets of two-column paper may be used for the balance sheet. List the assets on one sheet and the liabilities and owner's equity on the other sheet.

3. John Q. Public, a certified public accountant, has decided to go into business for himself. For the first month of operations, July 19____, Mr. Public has listed the following business transactions:

a. Mr. Public invested $22,500 cash in his new business.

b. Paid first month's rent, $375.

c. Purchased a word processing machine on account from the XYZ Equipment Co., $3,870.

d. Paid for the installation of a phone, $40.50.

e. Received $1,500 for services rendered to The Bigelow Loan Company.

f. Paid $2,250 to the XYZ Co. on account.

g. Received $1,125 for services rendered to the local Picken' Chicken franchiser.

h. Paid new secretary's salary, $750.

REQUIRED

A. Prepare a trial balance for July 31, 19____.

B. Prepare a balance sheet after Mr. Public's first month of business.

4.

ACE TRUCKING COMPANY
Trial Balance
August 31, 19____

Cash	$ 200	
Accounts receivable	5,000	
Supplies	2,280	
Prepaid insurance	1,440	
Equipment	7,720	
Truck	11,100	
Accounts payable		$ 200
Notes payable		6,600
S. Stern, capital		16,800
Truck rentals		13,040
Salary expense	6,560	
Rent expense	920	
Truck expense	1,120	
Utilities expense	300	
Totals	$36,640	$36,640

REQUIRED

A. Prepare an income statement for the Ace Trucking Co. for the month of August.

B. Prepare a balance sheet for the Ace Trucking Co. as of August 31, 19____.

CHAPTER 4

Recordkeeping—"It's Not Magic, But Neatness Does Count"

EVALUATING TRANSACTIONS

Because business accounting can be defined as the art (it's more like a fingerpainting than a Rembrandt) of evaluating and recording financial transactions, one needs something to evaluate. (It makes sense, doesn't it?) Therefore, the first step in the accounting cycle is the use of *source documents* to collect and classify business information. Source documents are a wide variety of business forms and papers that provide the initial information that starts the accounting cycle flowing.

Source documents include:

1. **Check stubs or copies**—Provide information regarding cash expenditures (i.e., payment of a utility bill).

2. **Receipts, cash register tapes, sales slips, or sales invoices**—Tells a business how much cash it took in from selling goods or services.

3. **Purchase invoices from vendors**—Give the facts about how much a business spends to buy goods and services (i.e., cost of goods sold).

To keep the evaluation of financial data as up-to-date and as accurate as possible, all source documents should be numbered and have at least one carbon copy. If a mistake is made, the source document should not be thrown away (that's a definite no-no). Write or stamp the word *void* on the document, and then try to do the following number correctly.

ACCOUNTS

When business information is recorded, it must be evaluated with respect to its effect on the basic elements of the accounting equation— assets, liabilities, and owner's equity (capital, revenue, and expenses). All financial transactions are classified in units called *accounts*. Every (not 99%, but 100%) asset, liability, capital, revenue, and expense item has its own account, which is kept in a book called a *General Ledger*. You can have several accounts on one page or several pages for one account, but the standard and accepted form (see Illustration 4.1) is shaped like a "T," hence the clever term *"T" account*. (And you thought accountants had no imagination.)

ILLUSTRATION 4.1
"T" Account

Account   (cash)   Account No.   (101)

Date	Explanation	Post. Ref.	Debit	Date	Explanation	Post. Ref.	Credit
(1)	(2)	(3)	(4)	(5)	(6)	(7)	(8)

Each account has eight basic columns divided into two sections. The left section is the *debit side* and the right section is the *credit side*. (*Note:* Debit = Left, and Credit = Right. Ergo, if someone says "debit the account," it means put the information on the left side.)

Columns 1 and 5 are the "date" columns. They are necessary because all financial information is recorded in chronological order.

Columns 2 and 6 are the "description" or "explanation" columns. They are used for any additional data that might facilitate understanding, such as a check number, an invoice number, or a specific item purchased.

Columns 3 and 7 are the "posting reference" columns. They indicate from where the information comes (i.e., J1 would indicate General Journal, page 1; P50 would indicate Purchase Journal, page 50). A check mark (✓) indicates that the data originate in the account (i.e., account balance).

Columns 4 and 8 are the "debit" column and the "credit" column, respectively. They show the cash amount involved in the transaction.

An account has two sides because various business transactions cause accounts to either increase or decrease. When an increase is shown on one side, a decrease must be shown on the other side. There must be an equal amount of debits and credits. Illustration 4.2* shows how increases and decreases affect the five accounting elements. I will use (↑) to indicate increase and (↓) to indicate decrease.

ILLUSTRATION 4.2

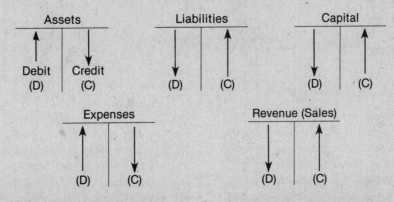

* It is important to see and understand how increases and decreases operate, so keep this diagram with you at all times. Laminate it for use in the shower.

Examples

TRANSACTION:

On October 1, 19____, S. Stern starts a business with $15,000 in cash. This transaction illustrates an owner's investment of an asset. When an asset (cash) is received (increases), you record the amount on the debit (left) side. At the same time, you make a contrasting credit (right) entry for the source of the asset, S. Stern, capital. Thus, you have equal debit and credit entries.

ILLUSTRATION 4.3

Cash

Oct. 1			15,000—			

S. Stern, Capital

			Oct. 1		15,000—

TRANSACTION:

On October 2, Mr. Stern purchases office equipment on credit from the ABC Co. for $2,000. This transaction illustrates the purchase of an asset on credit. When an asset (office equipment) is purchased (increases for cash or on credit, you debit the asset. When something is bought on credit (on account), you make a contrasting credit entry to show that a liability has been incurred.

Office Equipment

Oct. 2			2,000—			

Accounts Payable: ABC Co.

			Oct. 2	2,000—	

TRANSACTION:

On October 5, Mr. Stern purchases some furniture for $500. This transaction illustrates the purchase of an asset for cash. Just as in the previous example, the purchase of an asset requires that you debit the appropriate account. But since the furniture was paid for in cash, you credit the amount of another asset, cash.

Furniture

Oct. 5			500—			

Cash

Oct. 1			15,000—	Oct. 5		500—

Again, you have equal debit and credit entries. (*Note:* If the furniture had been bought partly for cash and partly for credit, two credit entries equalling $500 would be necessary.

TRANSACTION:

On November 1, Mr. Stern pays the ABC Co. $2,000 in payment for the office equipment. This transaction illustrates the payment of a liability. When a liability is paid, you show the decrease (payment) on the debit side. When cash is used as payment for a liability you credit the cash account to show the decrease.

Accounts Payable: ABC Co.

Nov. 1			2,000—	Oct. 2		2,000—

Cash

Oct. 1			15,000—	Oct. 5		500—
				Nov. 1		2,000—

TRANSACTION:

On November 2, Mr. Stern sells $1,000 worth of goods (or services) to the XYZ Co. for cash. This transaction illustrates the earning of revenue. When a sale is made and cash is received, you debit the Cash account to show the increase. When a sale is made, you credit the revenue (Sales) account to show the increase.

Cash

Oct. 1			15,000—	Oct. 5		500—
Nov. 2			1,000—	Nov. 1		2,000—

Sales

				Nov. 2		1,000—

(*Note:* If the sales were made on credit, you would have debited the asset account, Accounts Receivable: XYZ Co. for $1,000.)

TRANSACTION:

On November 3, Mr. Stern pays $100 on a telephone bill. This transaction illustrates the incurring of an expense. When an expense (telephone) is paid, you debit the amount of the expense. Because cash is paid, you credit the Cash account to show the decrease.

Telephone Expense

Nov. 3			100—			

Cash

Oct. 1			15,000—	Oct. 5		500—
Nov. 2			1,000—	Nov. 1		2,000—
				Nov. 3		100—

Simple and Compound Entries

For each of the foregoing financial transactions, there were equal debit (left) and credit (right) entries. A transaction where you have one debit and one credit is called a *simple entry*. An entry where debit or credit entries are divided between two accounts is called a *compound entry*. In compound entries, the total debits and credits *must* be equal.

Account Balance

The balance of an account is gotten by adding up the amounts on the debit and credit sides and subtracting the smaller amount from the larger amount. The difference is the *account balance*.

You should remember the following about account balances:

1. Assets have a debit balance or no balance.
2. Liabilities have a credit balance or no balance.
3. Capital has a credit balance or no balance.
4. Revenue has a credit balance or no balance.
5. Expenses have a debit balance or no balance.

The process of figuring the account balance and recording the amount is called *footing*. The account balance is shown in the "explanation" column on the correct side.

CHART OF ACCOUNTS

As part of good accounting practice, it is important to number all accounts so that anyone can know the authorized accounts and their proper designation (location) in the ledger.

All accounts should be kept in the ledger in numerical order. The *Chart of Accounts* summarizes the decisions made about what financial data is needed to aid in making future business decisions. As shown in Illustration 4.4, assets are listed first, followed by liabilities, capital, revenue, and expenses.

ILLUSTRATION 4.4

S. STERN & CO.
Chart of Accounts

ASSETS—101 to 199 *(All assets begin with "1.")*
Cash	101
Petty Cash	102
Current Assets	103–120 *(includes all receivables)*
Fixed Assets	150–170

LIABILITIES—201 to 299 *(All liabilities begin with "2.")*
Accounts Payable	201–220
Notes Payable	225–230
Taxes Payable	250–259

CAPITAL—301 to 399 *(All capital accounts begin with "3.")*
S. Stern, capital	301 *(In a partnership, each partner has separate accounts.)*
S. Stern, drawing	302

REVENUE (SALES)—401 to 499 *(Each revenue account begins with "4.")*
Sales	401–410
Interest Earned	411

EXPENSES—501 to 599 *(Each expense account begins with "5.")*
Salary Expense	501
Telephone Expense	502
Taxes Expense	510–515
Insurance Expense	520–522
Supplies Expense	525

RECORDING TRANSACTIONS

The Journal

The *General Journal* is a chronological, diary-like record of all business transactions involving money. It is the first step in the accounting cycle where debits and credits are used, and it is a mechanism by which amounts can be entered in the appropriate ledger accounts.

The simplest form of journal is one with two columns, debit and credit, which is shown in Illustration 4.5.

ILLUSTRATION 4.5
Two-column Journal

Date	Description	Post. Ref.	Debit	Credit
(1)	(2)	(3)	(4)	(5)
	Account to be debited			
	Account to be credited			
	Explanation			

Column 1 is the "date" column. All entries are listed in chronological order.

Column 2 is the "description" or "explanation" column. This column includes the name of the account to be debited (1st line), the name of the account to be credited (indented on 2nd line), and an explanation if necessary (3rd line).

Column 3 is the "posting reference" column. It gives the number of the accounts involved in the transaction (i.e., Cash 101).

Column 4 is the "debit" column. The amount to be debited is written on the same line as the account to be debited.

Column 5 is the "credit" column. The amount to be credited is written on the same line as the account to be credited.

I suggest that you use a bound journal to help keep this a permanent record.

Journalizing

Journalizing is the act of recording the significant information concerning each transaction in chronological order. Although journalizing does not mean that you are working for a newspaper, a properly entered journal will answer the same five basic questions that a well-written article will answer:

1. When? The "date" column shows month, day, and year.
2. Who? The "description" column tells which accounts are involved.
3. What or Why? The "description" column includes an explanation.
4. Where? The "posting reference" column tells where the information will be posted.
5. How Much? The "debit" and "credit" columns indicate the amount of money involved.

The General Ledger

The *General Ledger* is a book containing all the accounts necessary to supply the required information to complete the income statement and the balance sheet, and to aid in making future business decisions. The accounts are grouped according to the Chart of Accounts and listed by account number. Proper grouping of accounts will save you a lot of unnecessary thumbing through the pages. I recommend that you use a looseleaf binder so that pages can be easily added when necessary. When a ledger is started, it is difficult to judge how many pages a specific account will need. Use one page for each account and *don't* number the pages. Then you can easily slip in another page when required. (So if you went out and bought a hard-covered ledger, return it.)

Posting

Posting is the process of recording (entering) the information from the journal into the ledger. All amounts entered in the journal should be posted to the accounts at frequent intervals. The ledger is not a reliable source of business information until all transactions are posted. Because the accounts provide the data used in preparing financial statements, accuracy in posting is essential. Every transaction posted must include:

a. The date of the transaction
b. The amount of the transaction
c. The page in the journal from which the information comes

The above information is necessary for both debit and credit entries. Whenever you post, you must post *equal* debit and credit amounts.

Double-Entry Bookkeeping

While the original record of a transaction is a source document, the actual recordkeeping is done in two distinct places. First the information is recorded in a journal (commonly called *the book of original entry*), followed by a duplication of the same information in a ledger (book of accounts). Recording the information in two places offers a safeguard against embezzlement, and allows for a double-check against errors. A diagram of double-entry bookkeeping is shown in Illustration 4.6.

ILLUSTRATION 4.6
Double-Entry Bookkeeping

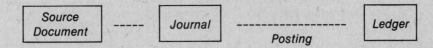

Bookkeeping (recordkeeping) is simple (and I don't say that to belittle bookkeepers or, as some are called, "Junior Accountants"). It is an important and essential function required in every business. Recordkeeping requires organization, neatness, planning and, for me, lots of coffee to stay awake.

Examples of Journalizing and Posting

The following examples of journalizing and posting should make it easy for you to see the relationship between the journal and the ledger.

TRANSACTION 1

On May 1, 19____, Jane Smith (I didn't want you to think I was both an egomaniac and a male chauvinist pig) invests $20,000 cash to start a business.

	Journal			Page 1
Date	Description	Post. Ref.	Debit	Credit
19___ May 1	Cash	101	20,000—	
	Jane Smith, Capital	301		20,000—
	Initial investment.			

			Cash					101
Date	Explanation	Post. Ref.	Debit	Date	Explanation	Post. Ref.	Credit	
19___ May 1	Opening entry.	J1	20,000—					

			Jane Smith, Capital					301
Date	Explanation	Post. Ref.	Debit	Date	Explanation	Post. Ref.	Credit	
				19___ May 1	Opening entry.	J1	20,000—	

(*Note:* Remember the credit line in the journal description is indented to make reading easier.)

TRANSACTION 2

On May 2, Jane Smith purchases a typewriter for
$600 on 30-days credit from the A-W Co.

Journal   Page 1

Date	Description	Post. Ref.	Debit	Credit
19___				
May 1	Cash	101	20,000—	
	Jane Smith, Capital	301		20,000—
	Initial investment.			
May 2	Office Equipment	112	600—	
	Accounts Payable: A-W Co.	201		600—
	Purchased typewriter.			

Office Equipment   112

Date	Explanation	Post. Ref.	Debit	Date	Explanation	Post. Ref.	Credit
19___							
May 1	Bought Typewriter	J1	600—				

Accounts Payable: A-W Co.   201

Date	Explanation	Post. Ref.	Debit	Date	Explanation	Post. Ref.	Credit
				19___			
				May 2	30 days.	J1	600—

TRANSACTION 3

On May 3, Jane Smith purchases a desk and
chair for $400.

Journal   Page 1

Date	Description	Post. Ref.	Debit	Credit
19___				
May 1	Cash	101	20,000—	
	Jane Smith, Capital	301		20,000—
	Initial investment.			
May 2	Office Equipment	112	600—	
	Accounts Payable: A-W Co.	201		600—
	Purchased typewriter.			
May 3	Office Furniture	113	400—	
	Cash	101		400—
	Bought desk & chair.			

Cash   101

Date	Explanation	Post. Ref.	Debit	Date	Explanation	Post. Ref.	Credit
19___ May 1	Opening entry.	J1	20,000—	19___ May 3		J1	400—

Office Furniture   113

Date	Explanation	Post. Ref.	Debit	Date	Explanation	Post. Ref.	Credit
19___ May 3	Desk & chair.	J1	400—				

In Transactions 2 and 3, assets that were purchased (increased) were debited. In 2, Accounts Payable was credited; in 3, Cash was credited.

Whenever you purchase something, you either pay (decrease) cash or incur (increase) a liability.

Special Books of Original Entry

For certain transactions that occur frequently in business, special books have been designed to facilitate the initial recording and the later translating of financial information.

Cash Receipts Journal

This book is designed for companies that are paid in cash for goods or services. Every entry requires a debit to the Cash account in the ledger.

ILLUSTRATION 4.7
Cash Receipts Journal

Date	Account Credited	Explanation	Post Ref.	Cash to be Debited

Cash Disbursements Journal

This book is designed for companies that pay bills for purchases in cash. Every entry requires a credit to the Cash account in the ledger.

ILLUSTRATION 4.8
Cash Disbursements Journal

Date	Account Debited	Explanation	Post Ref.	Cash to be Credited

Combined Journal and Cash Book

In my humble opinion, this is the best book for small businesses, especially those run in the home (full- or part-time). This book allows cash receipts and disbursements to be set aside from credit sales, purchases, or expenses.

The Cash account in the ledger is only used at the end of the month when you total the cash volumes and post the totals to the Cash account. The other accounts involved in the transactions are posted as usual, one entry per transaction.

ILLUSTRATION 4.9
Combination Journal and Cash Book

Page 1

Cash D	Cash C	Date	Explanation	Post Ref.	Other Accounts D	Other Accounts C
20,000—		1	Cash	✓		
			J. Smith, Capital	301		20,000—
			Initial investment.			
		2	Office Equipment	112	600—	
			Accounts Payable:			
			A-W Co.	201		600—
			Bought typewriter on credit.			
	400—	3	Office Furniture	113	400—	
			Cash			
			Bought desk & chair.			
1,000—		4	Cash	✓		
			Fees (sales)	401		1,000—
			Sold services.			
	600—	15	Accounts Payable: A-W Co.	201	600—	
			Cash	✓		
			Paid for typewriter.			
	25—	25	Telephone expense	502	25—	
			Cash	✓		
			Paid telephone bill.			
		29	Accounts Receivable—			
			ABC Co.	103	1,000—	
			Fees	401		1,000—
			Sold services on credit.			
$21,000—	$1,025—	31	TOTALS	✓	$2,625—	$22,600—
(101)	(101)					

To prove the Combined Journal and Cash Book, all debits and credits must be equal.

	Debits	Credits
Cash	$21,000	$ 1,025
Other Accounts	2,625	22,600
	$23,625	$23,625

When the totals are proved, you post the debit and credit totals to the Cash account.

				Cash				101
Date	Explanation	Post. Ref.	Debit	Date	Explanation	Post. Ref.	Credit
31	Monthly Total	CJ1	21,000—	31	Monthly Total	CJ1	1,025—

In the Combination Journal and Cash Book, (CJ), the double underscore under the totals under the other accounts indicates that these totals do not get posted. The individual amounts have already been posted to the correct account.

Trial Balance

After all transactions have been journalized and posted, it is necessary to check (remember, bookkeepers and accountants are only human like you and me) that no errors were made and that there were equal debit and credit entries. To do this, you figure out (prove) the balances in each ledger account and list these balances (debit and credit) on a *trial balance* in order of their account numbers. The trial balance, therefore, is a test of the ledger. The debit side of the trial balance must equal the credit side. Illustration 4.10 shows how ledger accounts are balanced and how a trial balance is prepared. Jane Smith's company will be used as an example.

ILLUSTRATION 4.10
Ledger Accounts

				Cash				101
Date	Explanation	Post. Ref.	Debit	Date	Explanation	Post. Ref.	Credit
19__ May 1	Initial investment	J1	20,000—	19__ May 3		J1	400—
May 4		J1	1,000—	May 15		J1	300—
				May 20		J1	250—
	$20,025—			May 25		J1	25—
			$21,000—				$975—

			Accounts Receivable: ABC Co.				103
Date	Explanation	Post. Ref.	Debit	Date	Explanation	Post. Ref.	Credit
May 10	$1,000	J1	1,000—				

			Office Equipment				112
Date	Explanation	Post. Ref.	Debit	Date	Explanation	Post. Ref.	Credit
May 2	Bought typewriter $600—	J1	600—				

Office Furniture   113

Date	Explanation	Post. Ref.	Debit	Date	Explanation	Post. Ref.	Credit
May 3	Bought desk & chair $400	J1	400—				

Accounts Payable: A-W Co.   201

Date	Explanation	Post. Ref.	Debit	Date	Explanation	Post. Ref.	Credit
May 15	Partial Payment	J1	300—	May 2	$300	J1	600—

Jane Smith, Capital   301

Date	Explanation	Post. Ref.	Debit	Date	Initial Investment	Post. Ref.	Credit
				May 1	20,000—	J1	20,000—

Fees   401

Date	Explanation	Post. Ref.	Debit	Date	Explanation	Post. Ref.	Credit
				May 4	T. Jones	J1	1,000—
				May 10	ABC $2,000—	J1	1,000—

Rent Expense   501

Date	Explanation	Post. Ref.	Debit	Date	Explanation	Post. Ref.	Credit
May 20	$250	J1	250—				

Telephone Expense   502

Date	Explanation	Post. Ref.	Debit	Date	Explanation	Post. Ref.	Credit
May 25	$25	J1	25—				

Now that you have all the balances, you list them numerically and compile a trial balance.

JANE SMITH CO.
Trial Balance
May 31, 19____

Account	Account No.	Debit	Credit
Cash	101	$20,025	
Accounts receivable: ABC	103	1,000	
Office equipment	112	600	
Office furniture	113	400	
Accounts payable: A-W Co.	201		$ 300
Jane Smith, capital	301		20,000
Fees	401		2,000
Rent expense	501	250	
Telephone expense	502	25	
Totals		$22,300	$22,300

Although the trial balance indicates that the ledger is in balance, there may still be errors, especially if the wrong account was debited or credited. For example, the Office Furniture account may have been debited instead of the Office Equipment account when Jane Smith pur- chased the typewriter. To reiterate: *Neatness and extreme care count.*

After the accounts have been proved by using a trial balance, the next step is to prepare Jane Smith's income statement and balance sheet. (Isn't this exciting?)

ILLUSTRATION 4.11

JANE SMITH CO.
Income Statement
For Period Ending May 31, 19____

Revenue:
Fees $2,000

Expenses:
Rent expense $250
Telephone expense 25

Total expenses 275
Net income $1,725

ILLUSTRATION 4.12

JANE SMITH CO.
Balance Sheet
As of May 31, 19____

ASSETS		LIABILITIES	
Cash	$20,025	Accounts payable	$ 300
Accounts receivable .	1,000	**OWNER'S EQUITY**	
Office equipment	600		
Office furniture......	400	J. Smith, capital	$20,000
Total Assets	$22,025	Net income	1,725
		Total owner's equity ...	21,725
		Total Liabilities and Owner's Equity	$22,025

ACCOUNTING CYCLE

Completing the financial statements is the final step of the *basic accounting cycle*. Illustration 4.13 shows how accounting information flows through the accounting cycle, supplying data and all the answers about the finances of a business.

As you can now easily see from the illustration, accounting is a step-by-step approach to understanding the finances of a business or an individual. In the chapters that follow, you will make use of the foregoing materials to expand your knowledge, find ways to save money, and aid in making business decisions.

Don't stop now—charge!

ILLUSTRATION 4.13
The Accounting Cycle

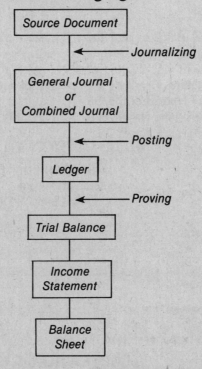

EXERCISES AND PROBLEMS
FOR CHAPTER 4

Recordkeeping

Exercises

1. Journalize the following transactions for the Jones Travel Agency. Then post the transactions to "T" accounts. After posting, prepare a trial balance from the account balance.

Transactions for July

July 1 Mary Jones organized the Jones Travel Agency by investing $85,000 in cash and a typewriter worth $1,000.
　　3 Purchased some office furniture for $3,000; 50% was paid for in cash and 50% was purchased on account.
　　6 Paid $500 for services rendered.
　　9 Paid rent, $350.
　 15 Paid employee for two weeks salary, $400.
　 17 Paid $1,000 on account for office furniture.
　 21 Sold services for $700 on account.
　 30 Paid employee for two weeks salary, $400.

Cash	Office Equipment	Land
(1) 57,000 (2) 30,000	(4) 11,250	(2) 30,000
(7) 2,000 (3) 12,500		
(5) 2,500		
(6) 8,250		
(8) 1,200		

Building	Truck	Accounts Payable
(3) 45,000	(5) 10,000	(6) 8,250 (4) 11,250

Notes Payable	T. Brown, Capital	Sales
(3) 32,500	(1) 57,000	(7) 2,000
(5) 7,500		

Salary Expense
(8) 1,200

Prepare journal entries for these eight transactions. Balance the accounts and prepare a trial balance.

Problems

1. Below is a trial balance for the Mary Jones Consulting Firm showing the ledger balances for the first 11 months of her accounting period.

2. The first eight transactions of a newly organized company appear in the following "T" accounts:

31

MARY JONES CONSULTING FIRM
Trial Balance
November 30, 19____

Cash	111	$ 3,634.28	
Office equipment	112	800.00	
Accounts payable	211		$ 191.45
M. Jones, capital	311		7,371.93
M. Jones, drawing	312	5,500.00	
Professional fees	411		11,990.00
Rent expense	511	2,200.00	
Telephone expense	512	225.60	
Electric expense	513	143.70	
Salary expense	514	6,600.00	
Charitable contributions expense	515	325.00	
Miscellaneous expense	516	124.80	
Totals		$19,553.38	$19,553.38

Transactions for December

Dec. 1 (Thursday) Paid December office rent in advance, $200.

1 Paid electric bill, $12.67.

2 Paid telephone bill, $16.85.

2 Received a check from Wagner Electric Co. for $500 for services rendered.

6 Received $400 from Wetterau Grocer Co. for services rendered.

7 Donated to the Heart Association, $25.

7 Paid for cleaning office, $7.25.

8 Received check for $400 from Nooter Corporation for consulting services.

12 Ms. Jones withdrew $350 for personal use.

15 Paid secretary's salary for the half month, $300.

16 Purchased office furniture on credit from Union Furniture Co., $600.

19 Paid for having office windows washed, $5.

20 Received $200 from Associated General Contractors for services rendered.

22 Paid traveling expenses while on business, $32.25.

23 Donated to the United Fund, $30.

26 Paid Union Furniture Co. $200 on account.

28 Ms. Jones withdrew $150 for personal use.

30 Paid secretary's salary for the half month, $300.

REQUIRED

A. Journalize the December transactions. For the journal, use two sheets of two-column journal paper and number the pages.

B. Open the necessary ledger accounts. Allow one page for each account and number the accounts. Record the December 1 balances and post the journal entries. Foot the journal.

C. Prepare a trial balance for December 31.

D. Prepare an income statement and a balance sheet for the entire year.

2. Plaza Parking System was organized on March 1 for the purpose of operating an automobile parking lot. Included in the company's ledger are the following ledger accounts and their identification numbers:

Cash	101	Parking fees,	
Land	121	earned	401
Notes payable	201	Advertising	
Accounts		expense	501
payable	202	Utilities	
Howard Cohen,		expense	503
capital	301	Salaries	
Howard Cohen,		expense	505
drawing	302		

Transactions for March

Mar. 1 Howard Cohen deposited $102,000 cash in a bank account in the name of the business, the Plaza Parking System.

2 Purchased land for $90,000, of which $54,000 was paid in cash. A short-term note payable (without interest) was issued for the balance of $36,000.

2 An arrangement was made with the Century Club to provide parking privileges for its customers. Century Club agreed to pay $660 monthly, payable in advance. Cash was collected for the month of March.

7 Arranged with Times Printing Company for a regular avertisement in the *Times* at a monthly cost of $114. Paid for advertising during March by check, $114.

15 Parking receipts for the first half of the month were $1,836, exclusive of the monthly fee from Century Club.

31 Received bill for light and power from Pacific Power Company in the amount of $78, to be paid before April 10.

31 Paid $720 to the parking attendant for services rendered during the month. (Payroll taxes are to be ignored.)

31 Parking receipts for the second half of the month amounted to $1,682.

31 Mr. Cohen withdrew $1,080 for personal use.

31 Paid $12,000 cash on the note payable incurred with the purchase of land.

REQUIRED

A. Journalize the March transactions.
B. Post the journal entries to ledger accounts.
C. Prepare a trial balance for March 31.
D. Prepare an income statement and a balance sheet in report form.

3. The Robert Brown Consulting Agency was formed with other companies to develop employee pension plans which will meet the complex legal and accounting requirements imposed by federal regulations for all pension plans. Some clients of the company pay in advance for advisory services; others are billed after the services have been rendered. The company adjusts and closes its accounts each month. On May 31, the trial balance appeared as follows:

ROBERT BROWN CONSULTING AGENCY
Trial Balance
May 31, 19____

Cash	$19,747	
Prepaid rent	4,425	
Office supplies	1,485	
Office equipment	9,396	
Accumulated depreciation: office equipment		$ 348
Accounts payable		1,425
Unearned revenue		18,900
R. Brown, capital		16,000
R. Brown, drawing	675	
Fees earned		14,250
Telephone expense	840	
Travel expense	1,020	
Salaries expense	13,335	
Totals	$50,923	$50,923

Adjustments

a. Monthly rent, $885.
b. Office supplies on hand May 31, $975.
c. The office equipment was purchased on January 1. The useful life was estimated at nine years.
d. Services rendered during the month and chargeable to Unearned Revenue (subscription basis), $4,350.
e. Pension advisory services (nonsubscription basis) rendered during the month but not yet billed, $840 (debit Pension Service Receivables).
f. Salaries earned by employees during the month but not yet paid, $345.

REQUIRED

A. Prepare adjusting entries.
B. Prepare an adjusted trial balance.
C. Prepare an income statement.
D. Prepare a balance sheet.

CHAPTER 5

The Desired Income Approach to Small Business— "Do It Right the First Time, and It'll Be Smooth Sailing"

Every week, dozens of small businesses fail throughout this country. This is no joking matter, because the great majority of the owners will never have a second chance to prove themselves as entrepreneurs. A general lack of comprehension regarding accounting procedures can surely lead any businessperson down the road to ruin.

The ability to plan, open, and then operate any business requires an understanding of the essential accounting statements. They represent the results of planning and management, and reflect the present financial status of a business. This matter is so important that no one* should take the plunge into business until he or she fully understands the relationships of the basic statements, their meaning, and their composition.

BALANCE SHEET RELATIONSHIPS

Illustration 5.1 serves as an example for the purpose of explaining the *balance sheet relationships*.

Current Ratio

Current ratio is a prime measure of liquidity. *Liquidity* is the measure of a company's ability to pay its debts by converting its assets to cash. It goes without saying that if a company doesn't pay its debts, it will not stay in business too long. (A warm personality is never sufficient to cover one's accounts or notes payable.)

Current assets are those assets which are in the form of cash or can be converted to cash within 90 days. (*Note:* Assets are divided into current assets and fixed assets. The distinction is made to aid management decisions.) *Current liabilities*

---

* Unless your last name is Rockefeller or Getty, or you have a need to waste your time, money, and sanity.

ILLUSTRATION 5.1

ABC COMPANY
Balance Sheet
As of December 31, 19____

ASSETS		LIABILITIES	
Current assets:		*Current liabilities:*	
Cash $2,780		Accounts payable.... $2,500	
Accounts receivable . 3,100		Notes payable 2,200	
Inventory 4,500		*Total current*	
Total current assets ... $10,380		*liabilities* $4,700	
Fixed assets:		*Fixed liabilities:*	
Equipment........ $6,200		Long-term notes	
Furniture 1,700		payable 3,000	
Truck 8,100		Total liabilities ..... $ 7,700	
Total fixed assets 16,000			
Total assets $26,380		**OWNER'S EQUITY**	
		[Owner's name], capital 18,680	
		Total liabilities and owner's equity $26,380	

are those debts which are due in a year or less. Current ratio is determined by using this formula:

$$\text{Current Ratio} = \frac{\text{Current assets}}{\text{Current liabilities}} = \frac{10,380^*}{4,700}$$

$$= 2.21$$

Sound management and planning demand that the current ratio be at least 2:1 ($\frac{2}{1}$). The ABC Company has a current ratio of 2.21:1; therefore, the company will definitely be able to pay its current liabilities.

Quick Ratio

Quick ratio is the primary test of liquidity. It is the relationship between only the most liquid assets (cash and accounts receivable) and the total current liabilities. Quick ratio is determined by using this formula:

$$\text{Quick Ratio} = \frac{\text{Cash plus receivables}}{\text{Current liabilities}} = \frac{5,880^*}{4,700}$$

$$= 1.23$$

The basic (conservative) rule is that the quick ratio should be at least 1:1. In other words, cash plus receivables should equal or exceed current liabilities. The ABC Company meets this "acid test" of liquidity because the company's quick ratio of 1.23:1 exceeds the minimum of this conservative rule. The quick ratio of 1.23 combined with the current ratio of 2.21 indicates that the present liquidity of this company is up to par.

---

* The numbers substituted into this formula come from Illustration 5.1, the balance sheet for ABC Company.

Working Cash

Working cash is the difference between current assets and current liabilities. Working cash is determined by using this formula:

Working Cash = Current assets − Current liabilities
= 10,380* − 4,700 = 5,680

The normal operation of any small business involves daily sales receipts, buying merchandise and supplies, and paying salaries and expenses. It is the working cash that provides the ability to meet all of these obligations and needs as they become due. There should be at least 90 days of working cash on hand at any time, since no one can always predict the ebb and flow of business all the time. (That includes me and I'm pretty smart.)

Proprietorship Ratio

Proprietorship ratio is the relationship between the owner's investment (capital) and the total assets used by the firm. Proprietorship ratio is determined by using this formula:

$$\text{Proprietorship Ratio} = \frac{\text{Capital}}{\text{Total assets}} = \frac{18,680^*}{26,380}$$

$$= 0.71 \text{ or } 71\%$$

A conservative minimum for proprietorship ratio should be 1:2 (50%). Only 29% (100% − 71%) of the total assets of the ABC Company are also debts (current and long-term liabilities). Because of this fact, the ABC Company will be able to borrow—for expansion or during hard times—on those assets which are free from debt. This works the same way as a homeowner taking out a second mortgage or trust deed on his or her house and property (Note: All companies should have credit available in case of a crisis.)

In connection with the owner's investment, you should become familiar with the term trading on the equity. Trading on too thin an equity is used to describe owners who have too little of their own money invested as compared with the creditor's capital (liabilities) used to finance the business. If the proprietorship ratio falls below 50%, this means that the creditors are supplying more of the firm's monetary needs (assets) than the owner is. Further credit may be impossible to obtain from either current loans, sales of securities, or other investors.

Unless variations from proposed, conservative rules can be justified with positive evidence, you, as a new business planner, would be wise to follow the rules of financial soundness as you make plans for your firm. Before resting on your laurels and adequate ratios, however, you should compare your data against the available statistics for the most efficient firms in the same line of business.

ILLUSTRATION 5.2
ABC COMPANY
Income Statement
For Year Ending December 31, 19____

Revenue:

Sales		$100,000
Cost of goods sold:†		
Beginning inventory, January 1, 19____	$15,000	
+ Purchases during 19____	45,000	
Goods available for sale	$60,000	
Less: Ending inventory, December 31, 19____	15,000	

* The numbers substituted into this formula come from Illustration 5.1, the balance sheet for ABC Company.

† Cost of goods sold is the expense of buying the goods that will be resold at a higher price (sales) to a customer. In a service business, revenue would be gross profit (margin).

Cost of goods sold . . . . , ...		45,000
Gross profit (margin) from sales		$ 55,000

Expenses:

Rent expense	$ 7,000
Salaries expense	15,000
Insurance expense	3,000
Advertising expense	1,500
Utilities expense	500
Telephone expense	1,000
Taxes expense	2,000
Miscellaneous expense	2,000

Total expenses	$ 32,000
Net income (profit)	$ 23,000

On an income statement, the gross profit (margin) and the total sales is its markup. The percentage of markup is the gross profit divided by total sales.

$$\text{Markup} = \frac{\text{Gross profit}}{\text{Total sales}} = \frac{55,000}{100,000}$$

$$= .55 \text{ or } 55\%$$

INFORMATION NEEDED TO PREPARE A PROJECTED INCOME STATEMENT

Four pieces of information are necessary to enable you to complete a *projected income statement*. They are:

1. The desired income
2. The average merchandise (inventory) turnover
3. The average markup
4. Profits as a percentage of total sales

The Desired Income

Every small businessperson hopes to receive both a return for his or her time spent working (in lieu of a salary) and a return on his or her investment (even a bank pays interest). The desired income should approximate the loss of salary plus whatever interest the money is already earning. Remember, money may be safe in a bank, but operating a small business may be hazardous to your financial health. Your decision as to the income you must have should not be emotional. Giving up your job and emptying your bank account is traumatic enough. So think, don't feel!

Even without any prior experience, planners can wisely determine their desired income by gathering the necessary facts from private and governmental sources. Trade associations, chambers of commerce, the U.S. Census, state industrial development departments, the Small Business Administration, and business service organizations like Dun and Bradstreet provide useful statistics.

The Average Merchandise (Inventory) Turnover

Turnover is the number of times the average inventory is sold each year. If a business carries an inventory of $15,000 and has a cost of goods sold of $60,000, the inventory turnover is 4 times per year. Turnover is determined by using this formula:

$$\text{Turnover} = \frac{\text{Cost of goods sold}}{\text{Average inventory}} = \frac{60,000}{15,000}$$

$$= 4 \text{ (turnover)}$$

Markup

The average *markup* is the percentage of the cost that is added to the cost to get the selling price. Most retail operations work on a markup of approximately 50%, which means the cost of buying the items is one-half of the sales price. If sales are $100,000, and the cost of goods sold is $60,000, then gross profit (margin) is $40,000. Markup is determined by using this formula:

$$\text{Markup} = \frac{\text{Gross profit (margin)}}{\text{Total sales}} = \frac{40,000}{100,000}$$

$$= .40 \text{ or } 40\%$$

Profit as a Percentage of Total Sales

Profit (income) as a percentage (%) of sales is the net income divided by the total sales. In a projected income statement, the desired net income is the beginning, not the end result, as is shown in Illustration 5.3.

STEPS FOR PREPARING A PROJECTED INCOME STATEMENT

A projected income statement is drawn up to see if the plans for a new business are financially sound. Illustration 5.3 is based upon these four pieces of information:

1. Desired income: $30,000
2. Turnover: 4 times per year
3. Markup: 35% of sales
4. 12% profit as percentage of sales

The steps are as follows:

Step 1—The desired profit is $30,000. You should insert this figure on the last line of the income statement, next to *Net income.*

Step 2—Through "investigation" profits have been found to average 12% of sales. To determine what the total sales are, you divide $30,000 by 12 to find 1% ($2,500) and multiply by 100 to find 100% of sales. The resulting figure is $250,000. You should insert this figure next to *Sales* on the income statement.

Step 3—Through "investigation" the average markup (for the competition) has been found to be 35%. You multiply the total sales of $250,000 by 35%. The resulting figure is $87,500. You should insert this figure next to *Gross profit.*

Step 4—The cost of goods sold is the difference between the total sales ($250,000) and the gross margin ($87,500), or $162,500. You should insert this figure next to *Cost of goods sold.*

Step 5—Since inventory turnover has been determined to be 4 times per year, and the cost of goods sold is $162,500, you determine the average inventory by dividing $162,500 by 4, which is $40,625. You should insert this figure on the projected income statement next to both *beginning and ending inventory.* (*Note:* If enlarged inventories are planned, adjustments may be made.)

Step 6—The goods available for sale is the cost of goods sold ($162,500) plus the ending inventory ($40,625), which is $203,125. You should insert this figure next to *Goods available for sale.*

Step 7—If the cost of goods available for sale is $203,125 and the beginning inventory for the year is $40,625, then the purchases for the year is $203,125 minus $40,625, or $162,500. You should insert this figure next to *Purchases*.

Step 8—Because the gross profit (margin) is

$87,500 and the desired income is $30,000, the difference must be operating expenses of $57,500. You should insert this figure next to *Operating expenses*.

ILLUSTRATION 5.3

Projected Income Statement
For Year Beginning January 1, 19____

Revenue:		
Sales	$250,000	(Step 2)
Cost of goods sold:		
Beginning inventory, January 1, 19____	$ 40,625	(Step 5)
+ Purchases during year	162,500	(Step 7)
Goods available for sale..................	$203,125	(Step 6)
Less: Ending inventory, December 31, 19____ .	40,625	(Step 5)
Cost of goods sold	162,500	(Step 4)
Gross profit (margin) from sales	$ 87,500	(Step 3)
Expenses:		
Operating expenses	$ 57,500	(Step 8)
(to be determined later)		
Net income (Profit)	$ 30,000	(Step 1)

This projected income statement tells the planner that for his or her plan to be feasible, all of the preceding factors must be in order. Otherwise, the business will probably fail.

After an income statement is prepared, every owner of a small business should ask himself or herself the following questions:

1. Is my markup too high or too low as compared to my competitors?
2. Is my consequent cost of goods sold too high or too low?

3. Are my expenses too high or too low?
4. Is my inventory adequate for my sales volume?
5. Is my rent the proper percentage of sales?

Trade statistics are available that will give you, as a new proprietor, comparative data with which to answer these questions. Studying statistics about other operations will reveal their strengths and weaknesses. All the answers are in the financial statements; analysis should be made of all key items on the balance sheet and the income statement.

STATEMENT OF ASSETS

Every new business requires a variety of assets with which to begin operations. *Cash* assets are needed for working capital (i.e., cash on hand) and for purchasing initial inventories and supplies. *Buildings* and *land* are expensive assets, which may be out of reach for most new firm planners. If this is the situation, they can rent or

lease these assets. *Prepaid expenses* (*insurance and supplies*) are assets that must be paid for prior to opening the doors to a new business. *Store fixtures, equipment, furniture,* and *delivery vehicles* are other assets which must be provided for the firm. Some can be leased or rented, like a typewriter, but others must be purchased.

One very common mistake most new proprietors make is underestimating the total asset requirements of the firm in the planning stage. Discovering your error later may be too late! Don't open your business "on a wing and a prayer!" To avoid this danger, you should analyze your firm by making a list of *every* asset the business will need and comparing this list with your available investment capital. Preparing a list of assets necessitates that you consider their cost and how they will be provided. If you've forgotten, assets are everything *owned* by a business.

Cash on Hand

How much cash do you need on hand?

A basic rule of thumb is "*cash should equal all expenses (including liabilities) for the period of one turnover of merchandise inventory.*" This is a conservative rule, but considering that small businesses are failing left and right, conservative thinking might save you from disaster. To determine the actual cash amount necessary, you should refer back to your projected income statement and divide the total expenses you'll need for one year by the average turnover (i.e., 4 times per year). For service businesses, you should conservatively start with cash on hand for three months, especially if your income is dependent upon payment of accounts receivable.

Inventory

You must be able to have enough inventory on hand to meet your contemplated sales. You can determine the amount needed by consulting with manufacturers, trade associations, or marketing experts.

Prepaid Supplies and Insurance

After studying your needs and legal requirements, you should shop around and discover the various kinds and costs of supplies and insurance. Every firm requires these assets.

Land and Building

Even if you plan to rent or lease the space you require, it would be a good experience to learn what it would cost to buy the land and the building. In the long run, it might be cheaper to buy, especially if you can afford to finance the down payment.

Renting or leasing space requires that you give the landlord cash as a deposit, security, or both. Before signing any lease for the space you have chosen as your location, consult an attorney. The amount of rent you pay should generally not exceed 10% of your total revenue.

Store Fixtures, Office Furniture, and Equipment

It is important that you understand your needs for store fixtures, office furniture, and equipment. Prices and terms can be obtained from suppliers. Check your competition and see how your plans compare with their set-ups.

Delivery Vehicle

A businessperson has the option of buying or leasing a delivery truck or car. If you buy, the truck or car becomes an asset. If you rent or lease, the cost for the same vehicle becomes a business expense.

OPENING DAY BALANCE SHEET

Planning for every new business should represent a careful study of your income needs, your expense requirements, and a conservative approach to balance sheet contingencies. The final step in financial planning is the *opening day balance sheet*, which is prepared *after* your research (i.e., market survey) has been completed.

The development of an opening day balance sheet requires that you make decisions on how each of the assets and/or the services is to be provided. These decisions will vary from planner to planner.

I will now invent a hypothetical proprietor and assign the following facts to assist him in making his decisions. The draft of his opening day balance will follow in Illustration 5.4:

1. Stanley Stern (who else?) has $50,000 to invest.

2. His Aunt Sally has offered to lend him $20,000 on a five-year note at 8% interest.

3. A manufacturer has offered Mr. Stern terms in this type of business if he can sell him most of the inventory. The terms are 60% down and 40% in 60 days with no interest charges. Mr. Stern will need an inventory of $50,000.

4. Mr. Stern has found a used delivery truck he can buy for $8,000, with $5,000 down and monthly payments of $200 per month.

5. Mr. Stern finds some slightly used office furniture and fixtures available for $2,500 cash.

6. The required store equipment can all be bought with ⅔ down and ⅓ due within one year. The total amount is $9,000.

7. Prepaid expenses (supplies and insurance) have been discovered to be $3,000.

ILLUSTRATION 5.4

S. STERN COMPANY
Opening Day Balance Sheet
As of October 1, 19____

ASSETS			LIABILITIES		
Current assets:			*Current liabilities:*		
Cash	$23,500		Accounts payable		
Inventory	50,000		(for inventory)	$20,000	
Prepaid expenses	3,000		Notes payable		
			(for equipment)	3,000	
Total current assets		$76,500	Total current liabilities		$23,000
Fixed assets:					
Equipment	9,000		*Fixed liabilities:*		
Furniture and			Notes payable		
fixtures	2,500		(to Aunt Sally)	$20,000	
Truck	8,000		Accounts payable		
			(for truck)	3,000	
Total fixed assets		19,500	Total fixed liabilities		23,000
Total assets		$96,000	Total liabilities		$46,000

OWNER'S EQUITY

S. Stern, capital   50,000

**Total liabilities
and owner's equity** $96,000

A check of Mr. Stern's balance sheet relation-ships is now in order.

$$\text{Current ratio} = \frac{\text{Current assets}}{\text{Current liabilities}} = \frac{76,500}{23,000}$$

$$= 3.33$$

This is much higher than the required 2:1.

$$\text{Quick ratio} = \frac{\text{Cash} + \text{receivables}}{\text{Current liabilities}} = \frac{23,500}{23,000}$$

$$= 1.02$$

This is in line with the required 1:1.

$$\text{Proprietory ratio} = \frac{\text{Capital}}{\text{Total assets}} = \frac{50,000}{96,000}$$

$$= .52 \text{ or } 52\%$$

This is in line with the minimum requirement of 50%.

If after extensive research, all the required data is financially sound, Mr. Stern is ready to plunge into his new business venture. Let's wish him luck!

EXERCISES AND PROBLEMS
FOR CHAPTER 5

The Desired Income Approach

Exercises

1. If you know the goods available for sale and the beginning inventory, how do you compute total purchases as part of cost of goods sold?
2. What are the key items (statistics) you must know to make a projected income statement?
3. Why is it important to have a current ratio of 2:1 and a quick ratio of 1:1 on the opening day balance sheet?

Problems

1. Mr. Green is planning to start a new clothing store. He has learned that the average markup in this line of business is 40%, profits average 10% of sales, and the turnover is 6 times per year. Mr. Green wishes to earn $25,000 in his first year of business. Prepare a projected income statement for Mr. Green.
2. Prepare a statement of assets to be used in a bakery. Assume the owner has unlimited financial resources.
3. Mr. and Mrs. John Q. Public desire to open a flower shop in Glenmore, California. The Publics wish to earn $50,000 in the first year. They have learned that profits are generally 25% of sales, the turnover is 52 times per year, and the average markup in the retail flower field is 50%. Prepare a projected income statement for Mr. and Mrs. Public.

CHAPTER 6

Accounting for Cash— "Don't Let Poor Accounting Procedures Dry Up Your Financial Resources"

In the foregoing chapters, you were shown (and, I pray, you learned) the purposes and uses for business accounting, analyzing various transactions, accounting jargon, financial statements, and the mechanics of double-entry recordkeeping. Various illustrations were given to illuminate the basic accounting cycle.

It is now time to turn your attention to the handling of, and the accounting procedures for, cash receipts and disbursements (that's income and outgo). For businesses that are service-, not product-, oriented, and for all consumer households, most transactions involve the exclusive use of cash. (*Note:* In accounting terms, cash includes currency, coins, checks, money orders, bank drafts and bank credit cards (i.e., Master-Card and Visa.)

Because no inventory is involved, a service business has no cost of goods sold. This type of business receives cash for services rendered (fees and salaries) and pays cash for its expenses upon receipt of its bills. A service business handles its expenses the same way a household does; therefore, consumers can benefit from a knowledge of the way cash receipts and disbursements are recorded. Usually any reference to cash receipts covers both the cash on hand (in a cash register, safe, or cookie jar) and the cash in the bank (checking and savings accounts).

CASH

Cash is an asset account that is debited (increased) when cash is received and credited (decreased) when cash is paid out. This means that the Cash account *must* have a debit balance or the business has no cash (and no business can survive without some cash).

Cash Receipts

It is vital to a service business (or a household) that an accurate and chronological record of cash receipts be kept. As the volume of receipts becomes larger, in both number and in amount, an accounting practice set up to reduce the danger of both mistakes and theft should be followed. When there are numerous receipts of currency and coin from customers paying cash for goods or services received, it is customary to use a cash register to record cash transactions,

before making bank deposits.

Cash Disbursements

A service business makes payments in cash or, as is the rule, by check. When a disbursement is made by check, the cancelled check or the check stub acts as the source document.

Recording Cash Transactions

In the preceding chapter I illustrated for you the recording of cash receipts and cash disbursement transactions in a two-column journal. This was done the same way as credit transactions (receivables and payables). If, however, you have all (or a majority of) cash transactions, the repetition involved in making large numbers of debit and credit postings from the journal to the Cash account in the ledger is time-consuming, tedious, and burdensome (boring busy work!). Later in this chapter, I will discuss the use of a special Combined Cash Journal, which can make this recordkeeping job easier.

Proving Cash

This is the process of checking to see whether the amount of cash (on hand and/or in the bank) equals the amount received by totalling the cash register tapes or the sales slips. Cash should be proved at least once a week, more often if the volume of cash transactions is large, or if you are worried about internal theft. (I don't want to sound like an alarmist, or a worrywart, but the greatest percentage of loss from theft in small businesses comes from employees, not customers. Proper cash controls may alleviate both the tension and the monetary loss.)

Cash Short and Over

This is a ledger account brought about for one of the following reasons:

1. The recording of receipts, disbursements, and cash on hand is filled with errors.
2. The count of cash or cash items (checks, money orders, travelers checks, credit card receipts) is incorrect.
3. A "shortage" or an "overage" exists.

Finding that cash is a little short (not enough) or over (too much) is not at all unusual for a business that deals in cash transactions. People do make mistakes. If it is found that a shortage exists, treat it like a disbursement and debit the account, Cash Short and Over. If you find an overage, treat it like revenue and credit the same account. If at the end of the fiscal year, the debit side (short) is greater, the difference should be recorded as an expense on the income statement. However, if the credit side (over) is greater, the difference should be recorded as revenue on the income statement.

PETTY CASH FUND

When all cash receipts are deposited in the bank and all usual disbursements are paid by check, your records of cash receipts and disbursements will happily equal the bank's record of your deposits and withdrawals. To pay for small unexpected disbursements (expenses), a small office fund, called the *Petty Cash Fund*, should be established. This fund eliminates the necessity of writing checks for small amounts, such as 50¢ to the mailman for postage due. To start such a fund, it is necessary to write a check for the amount of cash deposited in the fund, and record the transaction as in Illustration 6.1.

ILLUSTRATION 6.1
Petty Cash Fund

	Journal			Page 1
Date	Explanation	Post. Ref.	Debit	Credit
Dec. 1	Petty Cash	102	100	
	Cash	101		100
	Started fund, Check #150			

Cash	101		Petty Cash	102
	Dec. 1 100		Dec. 1 100	

(*Note:* Petty Cash is an asset account, usually found directly following the Cash account in the ledger.)

The check should be made payable to cash, or petty cash, and endorsed by the *one* person in charge of the fund. The Petty Cash Fund is a revolving fund, where the cash on hand plus all vouchers received (Illustration 6.2) equals the total amount originally charged to the fund.

ILLUSTRATION 6.2

PETTY CASH VOUCHER

No. _____   Date _____

Paid to _____
                                                    | Amount |
For _____ | |

Account to Debit _____

Payment Received: Approved by:

_____   _____

After the Petty Cash Fund has been established, it is a good practice to keep a record of transactions in a Petty Cash Record, which you can prepare yourself or buy at a stationery store. (*Note:* Petty cash payments are only made upon receipt of a voucher, and payments should be controlled by only one person.)

When the cash in the account gets low, another check equal to the total of the disbursements should be written. The transaction should again be journalized and posted to the proper accounts. Illustration 6.3 shows a page from a Petty Cash Record and gives a brief narrative of sample petty cash transactions. Following this illustration should enable you to conform your own Petty Cash Record to your individual needs.

ILLUSTRATION 6.3
Petty Cash Record

For Month, _____ May 19____   Page ___1___

Date	Explanation	Vou. No.	Total Amount	Telephone Expense	Postage Expense	Travel Expense	Delivery Expense	Misc. Expense	Account	Amount
May 1	Started fund $100.00									
3	Gas	1	10.50				10.50			
5	Stamps	2	15.00		15.00					
16	Long distance call	3	4.75	4.75						
27	Mr. Stern, personal	4	20.00						S. Stern, Capital	20.00
28	Washing windows	5	6.25					6.25		
29	Travel expense	6	11.25			11.25				
30	Truck maintenance	7	2.75				2.75			
			70.50	4.75	15.00	11.25	13.25	6.25		20.00
31	Balance		29.50							
31	Received in Fund		70.50							
	Total		100.00							

Transactions for May

May 1 Issued check no. 1000 payable to petty cash to start fund.

3 Gave Mr. Smith $10.50 to reimburse him for gas for truck.

5 Gave Marge $15.00 to reimburse her for a roll of stamps.

16 Gave Bill Jones $4.75 to reimburse him for call from home.

27 Gave Mr. Stern (owner) $20.00 for his personal use.

28 Paid window cleaner $6.25 for monthly cleaning.

29 Gave Mr. Stern $11.25 to reimburse him for travel expenses.

30 Gave Mr. Smith $2.75 to reimburse him for oil for truck.

(*Note:* To prove the Petty Cash Record, you foot [total] all the individual columns and add them together. This total must equal the total of the "Total Amount" column.)

BANKING PROCEDURES

A bank (you know, those places on almost every corner) is a financial institution that will accept your deposits, make collections for you, lend you money, and render other services. It is extremely important that all small businesspeople develop a relationship with a banker, because when credit is needed quickly, someone familiar with your situation can be of ready assistance. So do all your banking—business and personal—at one bank.

Checking Account

Today, 90%–98% of all payments are made by check. A check is a piece of commercial paper that is drawn on a bank and payable on demand. There are three parties to every check:

a. **Drawer**—the depositor who orders the bank to pay by writing the check

b. **Drawee**—the place where the drawer deposits his or her cash

c. **Payee**—the person to whom the check is written and who can demand payment by endorsing (signing his or her name) the check on the back

A check is negotiable for cash because it is in writing, it is signed by the drawer, it contains an order to pay, and it is payable on demand to the payee. (*Note:* Small businesses should get a rubber stamp for endorsing checks, which restricts payment to only one person [or company name], such as, "Pay to S. Stern Only.")

Deposits

All deposits should be made by using specially numbered and printed deposit slips, where checks are listed underneath currency and coins (Illustration 6.4). The carbon copy of this deposit slip is maintained in order to prove the Cash account.

ILLUSTRATION 6.4
Deposit Slip

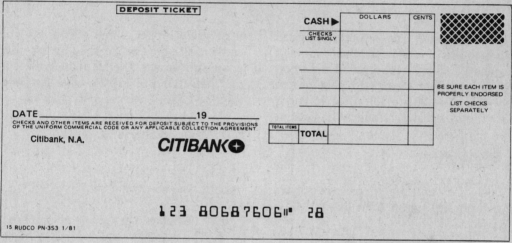

Dishonored Checks

A check that a bank refuses to pay is described as a *dishonored check*. The most common reason for checks being returned unpaid is *Not Sufficient Funds* (*NSF*). The bank usually will charge you a fee for handling such a check.

Most checks that are dishonored and turn out to be "bad" or "rubber" are not the result of any dishonest intent on the writers of the checks. Since checks are written by people, and some people cannot add or subtract, businesses have this problem. Either the depositor thought that he or she had enough money ("to err is human") or he or she expected one of the deposits to get to the bank in time to "cover" any checks that have been written.

Most banks have special accounts (i.e., "ready reserve" or "overdraft") available that work like credit cards and guarantee payment for a prescribed limit above the depositor's balance. Every small businessperson should have such an account. It only costs you if and when you use it.

Postdated Checks

Checks dated after the date of payment are called *postdated checks*. For example, a check written on May 1 may be dated May 16. The payee (receiver) cannot deposit it before May 16. This allows someone who presently has insufficient funds in his or her bank account the time to cover the amount of the check.

Generally, it is not considered good business practice to accept postdated checks for goods sold or services rendered. The reason is that it gives the payer time to cancel the check, forcing you to chase the payee for payment.

Night Deposits

If your business is open past normal banking hours and you deal in large amounts of cash receipts, you should use a bank that offers night deposit service, or at least a night safe with an opening on the outside of the bank. It is bad business practice (and it really screws up your accounting records) if your cash is stolen while it sits waiting for the bank to open.

Withdrawals

The amount you have deposited in a bank should be withdrawn only by check. This enables only the people authorized to sign checks to make withdrawals.

Checkbook

Businesses should use bound-numbered checks in the form of a book that has two parts (check and explanatory section) and a carbon copy that can be kept as a permanent source document. If a mistake is made while writing a check, *DON'T* throw it away! Either write *Void* on it or get a rubber stamp that prints *Void*. The same rule should be followed for any numbered source document. There's nothing more frustrating than trying to explain what happened to a missing check, invoice, or deposit slip.

Bank Records

Most businesses and many consumers have specific records and transactions handled by a bank. They include:

1. Accepting and recording deposits
2. Paying checks issued by depositors
3. Lending money to depositors
4. Collecting amounts for various kinds of commercial paper, such as bonds or notes receivable
5. Overcharge checking when depositor's funds are insufficient

The bank keeps an account for each depositor and mails a statement to each depositor every month. The statement shows:

a. The balance at the beginning of the period
b. The deposits received by the bank during the period
c. The checks honored by the bank during the period
d. Any other items charged to the depositor's account
e. The balance at the end of the period

With the statement, the depositor also receives all the cancelled checks honored during the period, together with copies of any items charged to the account.

Reconciling the Bank Statement

This is one of the most bothersome procedures involved in recordkeeping. However, when you receive your statement you should check it immediately with your checkbook records. This procedure is known as *reconciling*, and it has caused more divorces than interfering in-laws. The balance on the statement will almost invariably differ from the balance in your checkbook. Some of the reasons for the differences are:

1. **Outstanding Checks**—These are checks you issued, but were not presented to the bank for payment prior to the statement being compiled. By comparing the re-

turned cancelled checks and your check-book copies or stubs, you can determine which checks are outstanding.

2. **Deposits in Transit**—Although you might have made a deposit, the bank may not have recorded it prior to completing your statement.
3. **Service Charges**—These are the amounts the bank subtracts from your account for services rendered.
4. **Dishonored Checks**—Although you thought they were good, the bank would not honor them. Sorry!
5. **Errors in the Statement** (i.e., crediting your account for someone else's check).
6. **Errors in Your Checkbook**

(*Note:* Many banks offer *free* checking accounts. It's silly to pay them for making money with your money.) If you are unable to reconcile your statement even after Stern's "Easy Reconciliation Method" (Illustration 6.5), notify your bank immediately.

ILLUSTRATION 6.5
Bank Reconciliation Procedure

Checkbook:
Step 1—Compare cancelled checks to your records for possible mistakes in transposing numbers.
Step 2—Subtract service charges from balance.
Step 3—Subtract dishonored checks from balance.

Bank Statement:
Step 4—Add any deposits in transit.
Step 5—Subtract any outstanding checks.
Step 6—Check to see if any mistakes were made in statement (i.e., crediting wrong account).

Savings Account

Both businesspeople and consumers who keep part of their cash in savings accounts must record the interest paid as revenue in the journal and then in the ledger. The account is generally called Interest Income Earned.

ACCOUNTING FOR A CASH (SERVICE) BUSINESS

A cash business is one that records receipt of revenue and payment of expenses when cash is actually received or paid. This may mean that although services are given in one accounting period, the revenue will not be received and accounted for until the next period. In most cases, a professional person (i.e., lawyer, consultant, agent, and, yes, even accountants) has no revenue until he or she actually receives it. (You can't spend a promise to pay.) Business enterprises of this type are real estate, insurance, advertising, entertainment, and brokerage. Professional enterprises usually include law, medicine, dentistry, engineering, consulting, art, education, and last, but not least, public accounting.

Any property or service that is accepted as payment is treated as cash, based upon its fair market value. For example, a doctor can perform an operation on the owner of a tennis club, and, in lieu of cash, accept membership in the club as payment. Therefore, the value of the membership is recorded as revenue.

Exceptions to the Cash Basis of Accounting

One exception to the cash basis of accounting is the *depreciation* of long-lived assets (i.e., a car). If it is expected that an asset will be used over a period of years, the cost of the asset is allocated (divided) over its estimated life. The share of cost allocated for each accounting period is called *depreciation expense.*

Another exception is the use of prepaid ex-penses, which generally take the form of in-surance and supplies. In both insurance and sup-plies, an asset is purchased. As it is used, the amount used becomes an expense. At the end of the accounting period, even if there is still some insurance coverage or supplies remaining, the part used is listed as a business expense.

Combined Cash Journal

When a business records its receipts and payments when paid, it requires a great number of transactions going through the Cash account. A considerable savings of time, space, and energy can result by adding two columns to a regular journal for cash debits and credits. The regular "debit" and "credit" columns can be used for all other accounts. A journal with the special columns, "General Debit" and "General Credit," to handle any changes in accounts, is called a *Combined Cash Journal* (Illustration 6.6).

ILLUSTRATION 6.6
Combined-Cash Journal

For the Month of _____ 19____   Page ____

| CASH | | Check No. | Date | Explanation | Post Ref. | GENERAL | | Fees (Credit 401) | Salary Expense (Debit 501) | PAYROLL EXPENSE | |
Debit	Credit					Debit	Credit			Emplymt. Taxes	FICA

General Ledger

For service businesses, the standard form of account is used. The only change that occurs is that debit and credit entries to cash are recorded in the Cash account only at the end of the month.

End-of-Period Worksheet

To facilitate the preparation of financial state-ments, the making of any necessary adjustments (i.e., depreciation), and the closing of the revenue and expense accounts, which are tempo-rary (for one period only), it is common practice to prepare a *worksheet.* Illustration 6.7 demon-strates how all the necessary financial data can be accumulated on one sheet.

The first pair of columns, "Trial Balance," is used to show the trial balance, which was com-pleted after all transactions were posted at the end of the year. The second pair of columns, "Adjustments," is used to show how the use of depreciation expense and supplies expense works. Adjustments are used because no actual transactions occur, and the estimation of depreciation and the actual counting of supplies used is done after posting has been completed. After the adjustments have been added to, or subtraced from, the trial balance amounts, a new or "adjusted" trial balance is done.

ILLUSTRATION 6.7

S. STERN COMPANY
Worksheet
For Year Ending _____ 19____

ACCOUNT	TRIAL BALANCE		ADJUSTMENTS		ADJUSTED TRIAL BALANCE		INCOME STATEMENT		BALANCE SHEET	
	Debit	Credit	Debit	Credit	Debit	Credit	Debit	Credit	Debit	Credit
Cash	16,000				16,000				16,000	
Equipment	4,000				4,000				4,000	
Less: Accumulated depreciation		800		(a) 400		1,200				1,200
Furniture	1,000				1,000				1,000	
Supplies	900			(b) 500	400				400	
Notes payable		2,000				2,000				2,000
S. Stern, capital		6,600				6,600				6,600
Sales (fees)		30,000				30,000		30,000		
Salary expense	11,500				11,500		11,500			
Utility expense	2,000				2,000		2,000			
Advertising expense	1,000				1,000		1,000			
Rent expense	3,000				3,000		3,000			
Supplies expense			(b) 500		500		500			
Depreciation expense			(a) 400		400		400			
Total	39,400	39,400	900	900	39,800	39,800	18,400	30,000	21,400	9,800
Net income							11,600			11,600
							30,000	30,000	21,400	21,400

(a.) Depreciation for this year
(b.) Amount of supplies used during year

Financial Statements

The adjusted trial balance supplies all the information needed to compile an income statement (Illustration 6.8) and a balance sheet (Illustration 6.9) in account form. The difference between the financial statements on the worksheet and those written on the balance sheet is the division of assets (current and fixed) and liabilities (current and long-term).

ILLUSTRATION 6.8

S. STERN AND CO.
Income Statement
For Year Ending December 31, 19____

Revenue:

Sales (Fees)	$30,000

Expenses:

Salaries expense	$11,500	
Utilities expense	2,000	
Advertising expense	1,000	
Rent expense	3,000	
Supplies expense	500	
Depreciation expense	400	
Total expenses		18,400
Net income		$11,600

ILLUSTRATION 6.9

S. STERN AND CO.
Balance Sheet
As of December 31, 19____

ASSETS			LIABILITIES		
Current assets:			Notes payable	$ 2,000	
Cash	$16,000				
Supplies	400		**OWNER'S EQUITY**		
Total current assets		$16,400			
			S. Stern, capital	6,600	
Fixed assets:			Net income	11,600	
Equipment	$ 4,000		**Total owner's equity**	18,200	
Less:					
Accumulated			**Total liabilities and**		
depreciation	1,200		**owner's equity**	$20,200	
	2,800				
Furniture	1,000				
Total fixed assets		3,800			
Total assets		$20,200			

Closing Entries

Because revenue and expense accounts are temporary (for one period only), they must be closed at the end of the period. The opening day balance of a new period must be zero. Based on the trial balance in Illustration 6.7, a chart (Illus- tration 6.10) has been prepared to demonstrate how an artificial account called "Revenue and Expense Summary" can be used to handle the posting without the benefit of a business transaction.

ILLUSTRATION 6.10
Closing Entries

S. Stern, Capital 301			Revenue and Expense Summary 521			Sales (Fees) 401		
	6,600		(b) 11,500	(a) 30,000		(a) 30,000	30,000	
(h) 11,600			(c) 2,000					
18,200			(d) 1,000					
			(e) 3,000					
			(f) 500					
			(g) 400					
			(h) 11,600					

Salary Expense 501		Utility Expense 502		Advertising Expense 503	
11,500	(b) 11,500	2,000	(c) 2,000	1,000	(d) 1,000

Rent Expense 504		Supplies Expense 505		Depreciation Expense 506	
3,000	(e) 3,000	500	(f) 500	400	(g) 400

Explanation of Letters:

(a)—You debit the Sales account to close the account and credit the "Revenue and Expense Summary" account.

(b)–(g)—You credit each expense account to close it and debit each amount to the "Revenue and Expense Summary" account.

(h)—Represents the net income gotten by subtracting the debit balance from the credit balance of the "Revenue and Expense Summary" account. This closes this "artificial" account and the net income is credited to the owner's capital account.

ILLUSTRATION 6.11

S. STERN AND CO.
Post-Closing Trial Balance
January 31, 19____

Account	Account No.	Debit Balance	Credit Balance
Cash	101	$16,000	
Supplies	103	400	
Equipment	110	4,000	
Less: accumulated depreciation*	010		$ 1,200
Furniture	111	1,000	
Notes payable................................	201		2,000
S. Stern, capital.............................	301		18,200
Totals		$21,400	$21,400

Post-Closing Trial Balance

After closing the revenue and expense accounts, and before you put the books to rest at the end of the accounting period (year), it is important that you check to see if any mistakes were made. To check for mistakes, one final step is necessary; you should compile a *post-closing trial balance* (see Illustration 6.11). This trial balance does not include the now-closed revenue and expense accounts, and net income has been added to the owner's capital account.

In visualizing the accounting cycle, you can see closing entries and a post-closing trial balance are performed *as of the final day of the accounting period*, but, the actual recordkeeping may be done days or weeks later.

Well, that's the end of Chapter Six. But, before all you businesspeople out there go out and fire your accountants, remember one thing: Accountants are people, too. They also operate professional service organizations.

---

* Numbers beginning with "0" are used to indicate opposite (negative) entries for the prior account. Instead of crediting the equipment account for depreciation, you open a separate account and credit that. Other examples of "0" numbered accounts are *Sales Returns and Allowances* and *Purchase Returns and Allowances*.

EXERCISES AND PROBLEMS
FOR CHAPTER 6

Accounting for Cash

Exercises

1. On January 31, the Cash account for the XYZ Company showed a balance of $27,600. The bank statement, however, showed a balance of $34,800 for the same date. If the only reconciling items are a $2,400 deposit in transit, a bank service charge of $4, and some outstanding checks, what is the total amount of the outstanding checks?

2. John Cross, a trusted employee of Wilson Company, found himself in personal financial difficulties and carried out the following plan to steal $1,000 from the company and to conceal his fraud:

   a. Cross removed $1,000 in currency from the cash register; this amount represented the bulk of the cash received in over-the-counter sales during the three business days since the last bank deposit.

   b. Cross then removed a $1,000 check from the day's incoming mail; this check had been mailed in by a customer, Larry Jansen, in full payment of his account.

   c. Cross made no entry in the Cash Receipts Journal for the $1,000 collection from Jansen but deposited the check in Wilson Company's bank account in place of the $1,000 over-the-counter cash receipts he had stolen.

   d. In order to keep Jansen from protesting when his month-end statement reached him, Cross made a General Journal entry; he debited Sales Returns and Allowances and credited Accounts Receivable—Larry Jansen.

   e. Cross posted this journal entry to the two General Ledger accounts affected and also to Jansen's account in the subsidiary Accounts Receivable Ledger.

REQUIRED

A. Did these actions by Cross cause the General Ledger to be out of balance or the subsidiary Accounts Receivable Ledger to disagree with the control account? Explain.

B. Several weaknesses in internal control apparently exist in the Wilson Company. Indicate the corrective actions needed.

C. The Warren Company established a Petty Cash Fund of $150 on June 1. On June 20, the fund was replenished for the payments made to date as shown by the following petty cash vouchers: freight-in, $9.50; postage, $46; telephone expenses, $3.20; repairs, $31.70; miscellaneous expense, $22. Prepare journal entries in General Journal form to record the establishment of the fund on June 1 and its replenishment on June 20.

Problems

1. The information listed below is available in reconciling the bank statement for the White River Company on November 30, 19____.

   a. The ledger account for Cash showed a balance on November 30 of $7,766.64, including a $100 Petty Cash Fund. Petty cash should be transferred to a separate account. The bank statement on November 30 indicated a balance of $9,347.00.

b. The November 30 cash receipts of $5,846.20 had been mailed to the bank on that date and did not appear among the deposits on the November bank statement. The receipts include a check for $4,000 from a brokerage house for the sale of 150 shares of stock of the Axe Co., which cost $6,270. Neither the proceeds on the sale of stock nor the collections on accounts receivable ($1,846.20) had been

recorded in the accounts of the White River Company.

c. Included with the November bank statement was an NSF check for $220 signed by a customer, James Puddock. This amount had been charged against the bank account on November 30.

d. Of the checks issued in November, the following were not included among the paid checks returned by the bank:

Check No.	Amount	Check No.	Amount
924	$136.25	944	$ 95.00
940	105.00	945	716.15
941	11.46	946	60.00

e. A service charge for $340 by the bank had been made in error against the White River Company account.

f. A non-interest-bearing note, receivable for $690, owned by the White River Company had been left with the bank for collection. On November 30, the company received a memorandum from the bank indicating that the note had been collected and credited to the company's account after deduction of a $5 collection charge. No entry had been made by the company to record collection of the note.

g. A debit memorandum for $7.50 was enclosed with the paid checks on November 30. This charge covered the printing of checkbooks bearing the White River Company name and address.

REQUIRED

A. Prepare a bank reconciliation for November 30, 19____.

B. Prepare journal entries required as of November 30, 19____ to bring the company's records up-to-date.

2. I. J. Sverdrup, a general contractor, had a balance of $150 in his Petty Cash Fund as of June 1. During June, the following petty cash transactions were completed:

June 2 (Thursday) Paid for typewriter repairs, $3.25. Petty Cash Voucher No. 32.

6 Paid for long-distance telephone call, $3.75. Petty Cash Voucher No. 33.

8 Donated to the United Fund, $20. Petty Cash Voucher No. 34.

9 Paid garage for washing car, $2.50. Petty Cash Voucher No. 35.

12 Gave Mr. Sverdrup's son $5 (Charge L. J. Sverdrup, Drawing). Petty Cash Voucher No. 36.

14 Paid for postage stamps, $6. Petty Cash Voucher No. 37.

17 Paid for newspaper for month, $2.75. Petty Cash Voucher No. 38.

22 Paid for window washing, $3.75. Petty Cash Voucher No. 39.

27 Paid Parent-Teacher Organization dues, $5 (Charge L. J. Sverdrup, Drawing). Petty Cash Voucher No. 40.

28 Paid for car lubrication, $3.00. Petty Cash Voucher No. 41.

29 Donated to the American Red Cross, $25. Petty Cash Voucher No. 42.

30 Rendered report of petty cash expenditures for month and received the amount needed to replenish the petty cash fund.

REQUIRED

Record the foregoing transactions in a Petty Cash Disbursements Record, distributing the expenditures.

3. Debra Ramos is a fashion consultant. For her business records she uses a General Journal and a General Ledger ("T" accounts). Following is the trial balance of her business as of June 30, 19____.

DEBRA RAMOS AND COMPANY
Trial Balance
June 30, 19____

Cash	101	$ 7,268	
Office equipment	105	1,600	
Accounts payable	201		$ 380
D. Ramos, capital	301		14,742
D. Ramos, drawing	302	11,000	
Fees	401		23,980
Salary expense	501	13,200	
Rent expense	502	4,400	
Utility expense	503	286	
Telephone expense	504	450	
Advertising expense	505	650	
Miscellaneous expense	506	248	
Totals		$39,102	$39,102

Transactions for July

July 1 Paid July office rent, $400.
  1 Paid utility bill, $24.
  2 Paid telephone bill, $59.
  5 Paid N.Y. Post for advertising, $65.
  7 Received $375 from Mrs. A. Smith for services rendered.
  8 Ms. Ramos withdrew $200 for personal use.
 12 Paid salaries for first half of June, $1,100.
 13 Received $650 from Grace Stores for services rendered.
 15 Contributed to the Heart Fund, $10.
 16 Paid $200 on account to ABC Mannequins.
 20 Received $280 from Mrs. J. Carson for services rendered.
 26 Ms. Ramos withdrew $620 for personal use.
 28 Received $185 from Ms. A. Jones for services rendered.
 30 Paid salary expense for second half of June, $1,100.

REQUIRED

A. Journalize the transactions for July.
B. Open "T" accounts on ledger paper and post the transactions from the journal.
C. Prepare a trial balance for July 31, 19____.
D. Prepare an income statement and a balance sheet for July 31, 19____.

4. J. Pierpont Stern bought the Bailey Service Co. from Mr. Bailey's estate. On February 28, 19____, he prepared a trial balance for his new business.

STERN SERVICE CO.
Trial Balance
February 28, 19____

Cash	101	$ 17,500	
Accounts receivable	103	5,000	
Prepaid insurance	105	550	
Land	111	14,650	
Building	112	85,000	
Service equipment	115	30,000	
Accounts payable	201		$ 21,080
Notes payable	202		50,000
J. P. Stern, capital	301		81,620
Totals		$152,700	$152,700

Transactions for March

March 1 Paid telephone installation fee, $90.

2 Paid utility expense, $75.

3 Received $400 from Ames Bros., Inc. for services rendered.

4 Paid $2,000 on account to First National Bank.

4 Received $1,500 from Jones and Co. on account.

9 Paid $175 for advertisement in a trade journal.

12 Received $320 from H & H Builders for services rendered.

15 Paid secretary's salary for first half of March, $650.

18 Paid insurance expense for March, $110.

21 Received $450 on account from Jones and Co.

23 Received $280 from Boyce Bros., Inc. for services rendered.

26 Contributed to the United Way, $100.

27 Mr. Stern withdrew $1,200 for his personal use.

30 Paid secretary's salary for second half of March, $650.

REQUIRED

A. Open "T" accounts for all necessary accounts.

B. Prepare a trial balance for March 31, 19____.

C. Prepare an income statement and a balance sheet for the Stern Service Co. for its first month of operations.

CHAPTER 7

Accrual Accounting—
"Buy and Sell Now,
Pay and Receive Later"

Most businesses, if given the choice, would prefer to handle their accounting on the *cash basis of periodic income*. But firms that buy and sell merchandise (goods) are generally unsuited to this, and must use the *accrual basis of financial recording*. It may be observed that the cash basis is satisfactory for a merchandising business *only* if all three of the following conditions exist:

a. All merchandise purchases (inventory) are paid for in the same accounting period they are purchased.
b. Cash is collected for all sales in the same period they are made.
c. There are *no* unsold goods on hand at the end of the accounting period.

It is meaningless to attempt cash-basis calculations of income if purchases, sales, and payments for purchases and sales to customers are scattered over two or more periods.

The accrual method of accounting for purchases and sales takes into consideration that businesses have in their possession goods or materials for which no payment has been made. For example, suppose as the owner of a retail clothing store, you purchase $10,000 worth of jeans to sell. If you made up your income statement and balance sheet prior to paying for these goods, you would include them as part of your assets and any sales of the jeans would become part of your revenue. Nice, huh? But this would not truly reflect your company's financial position, unless you also listed the $10,000 as a liability (debt) in the Accounts Payable account. After paying the liability your Cash account would be reduced by $10,000.

If you have a relatively high percentage of receivables (from sales) and payables (from purchases) and want to know how you stand on a month-to-month basis, rather than waiting until the end of a period, the accrual method of accounting is for you. In this chapter all illustrations will relate to "Stern's Glad Rags," a mythical clothier.

PURCHASES

To record the purchases of supplies, raw materials, and finished goods (cost of goods sold), the first step is to use numbered *purchase order forms*. By ordering through purchase orders, you can maintain better control because all purchases are made and/or authorized by someone given sole responsibility and accountability for this function. Using purchase order forms can reduce mistakes, confusion, and theft because when goods are received, you can check that what you got is what you ordered. Anything else goes back.

Purchase Orders

They are available in many pre-printed lay-outs, but you should make sure they include:

a. Consecutive numbers
b. Your name and address
c. Carbon copies (at least original and two copies)
d. A statement that your order number must appear on all invoices, packages, etc.
e. Spaces to describe how goods should be shipped, date required, and terms of pay-ment (based on your credit rating)

Purchases Journal

As you receive *invoices* from your suppliers, you should check them against the goods re-ceived (from the purchase order), and record the following information in a *Purchases Journal* (Il-lustration 7.2) or in separate columns in a Com-bined Cash Journal (Illustration 6.6):

a. The date of invoice
b. The invoice number
c. The supplier's name
d. The terms of payment
e. The total amount

If necessary, you can have columns to distin-guish between purchases of supplies, raw mater-ials, and finished goods. (*Note:* Purchases should also be recorded in the General Journal [Illustra-tion 7.1].)

ILLUSTRATION 7.1
General Journal

Page 1

Date	Explanation	Post. Ref.	Debit	Credit
May 1, 19___	Purchases Accounts payable: XYZ Jean Co. Bought 50 pairs of jeans	511/PS1 201	500	500

(*Note:* Purchases are an expense and therefore have an account number that begins with "5.")

ILLUSTRATION 7.2
Purchases Journal

Page 1

Date	Supplier	Account No.	Invoice No.	Amount	Freight In	Supplies	Finished Goods
May 1, 19___	XYZ Jean Co.	201	150	500			500

(*Note:* The column "*Freight in*" (or sometimes called "*Transportation in*") is used to record any costs of shipping above the amount of the in-voice. This is generally paid to the shipper who prepays it to UPS, Parcel Post, Railway Express, etc.)

When you pay invoices (and remember to pay only invoices, not statements), you should record the payment in the General Journal or in a Com- bined Cash Journal having a column called "Ac- counts Payable—Purchases." At the end of the month, you just put the total of all your pur- chases in the General Ledger accounts—Pur- chases, Accounts Payable, and Cash.

Accounts Payable Ledger

If you use a large number of suppliers for your purchases, it might be necessary to add an *Ac- counts Payable Ledger* (Illustration 7.3). This will enable you to keep track of when your payments must be made and how to take advantage of any cash discounts offered for faster payment. Each one of your suppliers should have a separate ac- count and the Accounts Payable account in the General Ledger should only be used to record monthly totals.

ILLUSTRATION 7.3
Accounts Payable Ledger

Date	Invoice No.	Name of Supplier	Post Ref.	Terms	Amount	Date Paid	Check No.
May 1	150	XYZ Jeans Co.	J1	2/10, n/30	$500	May 30	251

(*Note:* In the terms column, 2/10, n/30 indicates that a 2% discount is allowed if the invoice is paid within 10 days or the full amount (net) is due in 30 days.)

Purchase Returns and Allowances

This ledger account is credited (to offset debits of purchases in the Purchases account) for the cost of any merchandise returned to suppliers or for any allowances received from suppliers which decrease the cost of the goods purchased. This account should have a number beginning "05" to show that it offsets an expense account, Pur- chases, and you should list it directly after Pur- chases in the Chart of Accounts. There should be an offsetting debit to the Account Payable ac- count for the decrease in cost. If returns and allowances are large in proportion to purchases, a weakness in your purchasing operation is indicated.

SALES

To state the obvious, it is necessary for any firm involved in merchandise to make sales in order to eventually make profits. Therefore, since sales are the basis of any business, it is necessary and desirable to have a recording system that in- forms you about:

a. How much you're selling
b. To whom you're selling
c. How goods are shipped
d. When and how payments were received

Sales Invoice

When you sell services or merchandise to a customer who does not immediately pay by cash or bank credit card, it is necessary to send the customer a bill or *invoice*. Invoices should have:

a. Consecutive numbers
b. Name and address of firm
c. Carbon copies
d. Method of shipment

e. Terms of payment
f. Price per item
g. Total amount or "extension"
h. Description of the items

Invoices sometimes require two addresses, one where items are to be shipped, and one where the invoice is to be sent.

Sales Journal

A *Sales Journal* is a useful tool to record the sales of merchandise on account instead of adding a column to a Combined Cash Journal. A Sales Journal is also a practical way to break down and distinguish sales either by department or by product line. This in turn will help you determine which departments or product lines should be expanded and which should be reduced. Illustrations 7.4 and 7.5 show the recording of a sales transaction for the ABC Co. (Sound familiar?) For a retail business that collects state sales tax, a Sales Journal with additional columns for sales tax is necessary (see Illustration 7.6).

ILLUSTRATION 7.4
General Journal

Page 2

Date	Explanation	Post. Ref.	Debit	Credit
May 1	Accounts receivable: J. Smith	103	500	
	Sales: Dept. B	401		500
	Sold 50 pairs of jeans			

ILLUSTRATION 7.5
Sales Journal

Page 2

Date	Invoice No.	Customer Name	Amount	Dept. A	Dept. B
May 1	150	J. Smith	500		500

ILLUSTRATION 7.6
Sales Journal with Sales Tax

Date	Invoice No.	Customer Name	Total Amount	Sales Tax	Dept. A	Dept. B
May 1	150	J. Smith	530	30*		500

* In a state like California, where sales tax is 6%, only $500 of the total $530 is recorded as sales. The sales tax collected is recorded in an account called Sales Tax Payable until the amount is sent to the state.

When you receive payments, you should record the amount in either the General Journal or the Combined Cash Journal. The total amount received should be debited to the ledger account once a month. Total sales should also be recorded in the ledger account once a month.

Accounts Receivable Ledger

If your company makes a large percentage of its sales on credit (account), it is a good idea for you to set up an *Accounts Receivable Ledger* (Illustration 7.7). This will help you keep an up-to-date record of sales and payments for each individual customer. At the end of the month, you make one entry for the total accounts receivable to the Accounts Receivable account in the ledger.

ILLUSTRATION 7.7
Accounts Receivable Ledger

Date	Customer Name	Invoice No.	Total Amount	Sales Tax	Dept. A	Dept. B	Date Paid
May 1	J. Smith	150	$530	30		$500	May 30

Sales Returns and Allowances

The *Sales Returns and Allowances* account is debited to offset the credits made in the Sales account, and reflects the selling price of any merchandise returned by customers or for any allowances made to customers that decrease the selling price of the merchandise sold. The offsetting credit should be to the Accounts Receivable account if the goods were sold on account or to the Cash account if the sale was originally made for cash. The account number should begin with "04" to show that it offsets a revenue account. You should list it directly under Sales on the Chart of Accounts.

Sales Discounts

If you allow your customers to take a cash discount for early payment of invoices (i.e., 2/10, n/30), it is necessary to record the transaction as follows: When you receive payment, credit the *entire* invoice amount to the Accounts Receivable account, and then debit the difference (discount) to a separate account called Sales Discounts. This account should also have an account number that begins with "04." You should list it beneath Sales Returns and Allowances on the Chart of Accounts.

FINANCIAL STATEMENTS

When purchases and sales are bought on account, payments are not always made in the same period as the initial transactions. The amounts of receivables (assets) and payables (liabilities) should be included in the income statement (Illustration 7.8), although no cash has changed hands. There is no guarantee that a business will collect all its receivables, nor pay its liabilities for its purchases. I don't think any of you will be shocked to learn that some businesses, actually many businesses, go bankrupt.

ILLUSTRATION 7.8

STERN'S GLAD RAGS
Income Statement
For Year Ending December 31, 19____

Revenue:		
Sales, Dept. A	$200,000	
Sales, Dept. B	195,000	
Total Sales		$395,000
Cost of Goods Sold:		
Beginning inventory, January 1, 19____	45,000	
+ Purchases during year	185,000	
Goods available for sale	230,000	
Less: Ending inventory, December 31, 19____	25,000	
Cost of goods sold		205,000
Gross profit (margin) from sales		$190,000
Expenses:		
Salaries expense	$ 55,000	
Rent expense	45,000	
Utilities expense	7,000	
Advertising expense	1,500	
Insurance expense	2,500	
Supplies expense	2,000	
Total expenses		113,000
Net income		$ 77,000

If Mr. Stern does receive cash for all his sales and he does pay for all his purchases, then his balance sheet (Illustration 7.9) is an absolutely true reflection of operations for the accounting period. A balance sheet also reflects the impact of receivables and payables on the financial status of a company. Although a company may not be paid for its receivables (from sales), it is still liable for its debts (payables).

ILLUSTRATION 7.9

STERN'S GLAD RAGS
Balance Sheet
As of December 31, 19____

ASSETS	LIABILITIES
Current assets:	*Current liabilities:*
Cash $37,000	Accounts payable . $14,000
Accounts	Notes payable 8,000
receivable 17,000	
Supplies 4,500	Total current liabilities . $ 22,000
Inventory 25,000	
	Fixed liabilities:
Total current assets . . . $ 83,500	Contracts payable 5,000
Fixed assets:	Total liabilities $27,000
Store equipment . . $11,500	
Furniture 8,000	**OWNER'S EQUITY**
Fixtures 19,000	
	S. Stern, capital $18,000
Total fixed assets 38,500	Net income 77,000*
Total assets $122,000	Total owner's equity . 95,000
	Total liabilities and owner's equity $122,000

In these last two chapters, I have discussed accounting procedures for cash-based businesses and for accrual-based businesses. The major difference is seen in the cost of goods sold section of the income statement, where current receivables and payables are reflected. I believe you now have sufficient data to handle the recording and translating of financial transactions for either type of business or household.

* Again, this $77,000 reflects receivables and payables. Mr. Stern better not go out and buy an expensive car for that money.

EXERCISES AND PROBLEMS
FOR CHAPTER 7

Accrual Accounting

Exercises

1. Certain key figures from an income statement for two successive years are:

	Year 2	Year 1
Sales	$300,000	$220,000
Cost of goods sold	220,000	148,000
Operating expenses	56,000	52,800

a. The net income increased from $_____
in year 1 to $_____ in year 2.
b. The net income as a percent of sales was
_____% in year 1 and increased to
_____% in year 2.
c. The gross margin on sales increased from
$_____ to $_____.

2. During June, Bank Company made sales of
goods on credit amounting to $309,000, of
which $235,000 remained uncollected at the
end of June. Sales for cash during June
amounted to $39,500, and an additional

$169,000 was received in payment for goods
sold in prior months. Also, during June, the
Bank Company borrowed $31,000 cash from
the bank. What was Bank Company's total
revenue for the month of June?

Problems

1. The Boxman Company closes its accounts
annually on June 30. After all adjustments
were made on June 30, 1980, the adjusted
trial balance was prepared.

BOXMAN COMPANY
Adjusted Trial Balance
June 30, 1980

Cash	$ 49,300
Accounts receivable	43,000
Notes receivable	31,650
Prepaid insurance	2,143
Supplies	3,120

68

Inventory (June 30, 1979)	67,350	
Furniture and fixtures	45,000	
Accumulated depreciation: Furniture and fixtures		$ 2,650
Accounts payable		19,300
Notes payable		15,000
J. Boxman, capital		95,883
J. Boxman, drawing	19,500	
Sales		720,000
Sales returns and allowances	9,300	
Purchases	470,000	
Purchase returns and allowances		4,450
Salary expense	89,000	
Rent expense	20,000	
Depreciation expense	2,650	
Supplies expense	3,450	
Insurance expense	1,820	
Totals	$857,283	$857,283

The inventory as of June 30, 1980 was determined to be $68,463.

REQUIRED

A. Prepare an income statement and a balance sheet as of June 30, 1980.

B. Prepare the necessary "T" accounts to show the closing of accounts on June 30, 1980.

2. Jonathan Clothiers, a wholesale business, prepared a trial balance on September 30, 1980.

JONATHAN CLOTHIERS
Trial Balance
September 30, 1980

Cash	101	$ 12,800	
Accounts receivable	103	54,400	
Prepaid insurance	111	1,728	
Supplies		4,544	
Inventory (Sept. 30, 1979)	121	115,200	
Land	130	64,000	
Building	131	160,000	
Furniture and fixtures	135	38,400	
Accounts payable	201		$ 90,592
T. Jonathan, capital	301		272,000
T. Jonathan, drawing	302	24,000	
Sales	401		624,800
Sales returns and allowances	041	12,800	
Purchases	501	371,200	
Purchase returns and allowances	051		9,088
Transportation-In	502	15,424	
Salary expense	503	20,016	
Delivery expense	504	5,600	
Property tax expense	505	1,600	
Commissions expense	506	94,768	
Totals		$996,480	$996,480

A physical inventory taken after September 30, 1980 showed that merchandise on hand was $92,800.

Adjustments

a. Property taxes accrued but not recorded, $2,880.

b. Supplies on hand (not used), $1,344.

c. Expired insurance, $896.

d. Depreciation on land and building, 10%.

REQUIRED

A. Prepare a worksheet, including columns for adjustments, adjusted trial balance, income statement, and balance sheet.

B. Prepare an income statement and a balance sheet in account form.

C. Prepare "T" accounts for the necessary closing entries.

3. Mr. James Ward owns a video game and pinball machine arcade. Following is a reproduction of Mr. Ward's trial balance for the fiscal year ended June 30, 19____.

JAMES WARD'S ARCADE
Trial Balance
For the Year Ending June 30, 19____

Cash	101	$ 25,482	
Accounts receivable	103	14,776	
Supplies	105	2,608	
Prepaid insurance	106	3,600	
Prepaid advertising	107	1,800	
Land	111	10,000	
Building	112	200,000	
Accumulated depreciation:			
Building	012		$ 28,000
Equipment	120	250,000	
Accumulated depreciation:			
equipment	020		44,000
Accounts payable	201		28,634
Notes payable	202		140,000
J. Ward, capital	301		121,626
J. Ward, drawing	302	48,000	
Sales	401		1,231,934
Salary expense	501	754,228	
Advertising expense	502	28,600	
Utility expense	503	84,400	
Maintenance expense	504	162,600	
Miscellaneous expense	505	20,400	
Totals		$1,606,494	$1,606,494

REQUIRED

A. Prepare a ten-column worksheet after making the necessary entries to record the following adjustments:

a. Accrued salary expense, $7,934.

b. Expired advertising, $1,800.

c. An unpaid utility bill, $1,400.

d. Depreciation expenses: building, $9,600; equipment, $22,000.

e. Expired insurance, $3,000.

f. Assessed property taxes, $2,000.

B. Prepare an income statement and a balance sheet for the year ending June 30, 19____.

C. Prepare closing entries and a post-closing trial balance.

4. After seeing a trial balance for the Presidential Trading Company, Stanley Stern is interested in buying the firm. But first, Mr. Stern wants to see additional data for the end of the year.

PRESIDENTIAL TRADING COMPANY
Trial Balance
For Year Ending December 31, 19____

Cash	101	$ 5,050	
Accounts receivable	103	24,830	
Inventory	105	71,400	
Supplies	110	3,800	
Prepaid insurance	111	4,800	
Store equipment	115	51,300	
Accumulated depreciation:			
Store equipment	015		$ 24,300
Accounts payable	201		38,950
A. Lincoln, capital	301		161,350
A. Lincoln, drawing	302	24,000	
Sales	401		371,250
Sales returns and allowances	041	4,690	
Sales discounts	042	3,790	
Purchases	501	250,400	
Purchase returns and allowances	051		3,150
Purchase discounts	052		4,900
Transportation expense	502	10,400	
Salary expense	503	64,600	
Rent expense	504	48,000	
Other selling expense	505	32,910	
Utilities expense	506	3,930	
Totals		$603,900	$603,900

REQUIRED

A. Prepare a ten-column worksheet after making the necessary entries to make the following adjustments:

  a. Year-ending inventory, $72,600.
  b. Depreciation expense: store equipment, $4,050.
  c. Expired insurance, $2,400.
  d. Accrued salary expense, $950.
  e. Supplies still on-hand, $1,800.

B. Prepare an income statement and a balance sheet.
C. Prepare closing entries.
D. Prepare all balance sheet ratios to illustrate the company's financial condition.

CHAPTER 8

Payroll—
"They Are Depending on You!"

As soon as you hire employees to work in your business (or household*), you automatically become responsible for compliance with various local, state, and federal laws which require you to withhold income and social security taxes from salaries and wages, pay the employer's share of social security and unemployment taxes, and provide your employees with worker's compensation and disability insurance. There are also voluntary payroll functions that include withholding income for life insurance, health and dental insurance, pension and profit-sharing funds, payroll savings plans, and other sundry items like union dues, charity, or child support.

Now, before you panic and start cursing about all that "blankety-blank" paperwork, read on and discover that it's not all that difficult. To aid you in this task, you can use your employer's tax guide from the Internal Revenue Service and similar handbooks from your state and local governments. You can also use my superb recommendations to overcome your doubts and insure your full compliance with all the applicable withholding, payment, and filing requirements. (*Note:* Accurate accounting for employees' earnings preserves the legal and moral right of each worker to be paid according to his or her employment contract and the laws governing such contracts.)

EMPLOYEE EARNINGS AND DEDUCTIONS

After you hire a new employee, your first step in determining the amount to pay your employee is to calculate the amount of his or her total or gross earnings for the *pay period*. The pay period is either one week, two weeks, semi-monthly, or monthly. Each new employee should fill out a *W-4 Form* (Illustration 8.1) on or before his or her first day of work. As an employer, you must know the following about your employee:

a. Social Security number
b. Total exemptions claimed
c. Address
d. Marital status

New employees who are exempt from withholding taxes must fill out a *W-4E Form*. Employees should also complete city and state withholding exemption certificates or both, if applicable.

---

* Yes, you are required to fill out tax forms for household help, too. That includes maids, butlers, gardeners and part-time help.

ILLUSTRATION 8.1
Employee Withholding Certificate

Form W-4 (Rev. May 1977) Department of the Treasury Internal Revenue Service	**Employee's Withholding Allowance Certificate** (Use for Wages Paid After May 31, 1977) This certificate is for income tax withholding purposes only. It will remain in effect until you change it. If you claim exemption from withholding, you will have to file a new certificate on or before April 30 of next year.

Type or print your full name   Your social security number

Home address (number and street or rural route)

Marital Status

☐ Single   ☐ Married

☐ Married, but withhold at higher Single rate

City or town, State, and ZIP code

Note: *If married, but legally separated, or spouse is a nonresident alien, check the single block.*

1 Total number of allowances you are claiming . . . .

2 Additional amount, if any, you want deducted from each pay (if your employer agrees) . . . . $

3 I claim exemption from withholding (see instructions). Enter "Exempt" . . . .

Under the penalties of perjury, I certify that the number of withholding exemptions and allowances claimed on this certificate does not exceed the number to which I am entitled. If claiming exemption from withholding, I certify that I incurred no liability for Federal income tax for last year and that I anticipate that I will incur no liability for Federal income tax for this year.

Signature ▶---   Date ▶-------------------------------, 19---------

---
Detach along this line

▲   *Give the top part of this form to your employer; keep the lower part for your records and information*   ▲

Instructions

The explanatory material below will help you determine your correct number of withholding allowances, and will assist you in completing the Form W-4 at the top of this page.

Avoid Overwithholding or Underwithholding

By claiming the number of withholding allowances you are entitled to, you can fit the amount of tax withheld from your wages to your tax liability. In addition to the allowances for personal exemptions to be claimed in item (a), be sure to claim any additional allowances you are entitled to in item (b), "Special withholding allowance," and item (c), "Allowance(s) for credit(s) and/or deduction(s)." While you may claim these allowances on Form W-4 for withholding purposes, you may not claim them under "Exemptions" on your tax return Form 1040 or Form 1040A.

You may claim the special withholding allowance if you are single with only one employer, or married with only one employer and your spouse is not employed. If you have unusually large itemized deductions, an alimony deduction, or credit(s) for child care expenses, earned income, or credit for the elderly, you may claim additional allowances to avoid having too much income tax withheld from your wages. Please note that alimony is no longer an itemized deduction, but rather is an adjustment to gross income. It may be to your benefit to take the standard deduction in lieu of itemizing deductions because of this change.

If you and your spouse are both employed or you have more than one employer, you should make sure that enough has been withheld. If you find that you need more withholding, claim fewer exemptions or ask for additional withholding or request to be withheld at the higher "Single" status. If you are currently claiming additional withholding allowances based on itemized deductions, check the worksheet on the back to see that you are claiming the proper number of allowances.

How Many Withholding Allowances May You Claim?

Use the schedule below to determine the number of allowances you may claim for tax withholding purposes. In determining the number, keep in mind these points: if you are single and hold more than one job, you may not claim the same allowances with more than one employer at the same time; or, if you are married and both you and your spouse are employed, you may not both claim the same allowances with your employers at the same time. A nonresident alien, other than a resident of Canada, Mexico, or Puerto Rico, may claim only one personal allowance.

Completing Form W-4

If you find you are entitled to one or more allowances in addition to those you are now claiming, increase your number of allowances by completing the form above and filing it with your employer. If the number of allowances you previously claimed decreases, you must file a new Form W-4 within 10 days. (If you expect to owe more tax than will be withheld, you may increase your withholding by claiming fewer or "0" allowances on line 1, or by asking for additional withholding on line 2, or both.)

You may claim exemption from withholding of Federal income tax if you had no liability for income tax for last year, and you anticipate that you will incur no liability for income tax for this year. You may not claim exemption if your joint or separate return shows tax liability before the allowance of any credit for income tax withheld. If you are exempt, your employer will not withhold Federal income tax from your wages. However, social security tax will be withheld if you are covered by the Federal Insurance Contributions Act.

You must revoke this exemption (1) within 10 days from the time you anticipate you will incur income tax liability for the year or (2) on or before December 1 if you anticipate you will incur Federal income tax liability for the next year. If you want to stop or are required to revoke this exemption, you must file a new Form W-4 with your employer showing the number of withholding allowances you are entitled to claim. This certificate for exemption from withholding will expire on April 30 of next year unless a new Form W-4 is filed before that date.

The Following Information is Provided in Accordance with the Privacy Act of 1974

The Internal Revenue Code requires every employee to furnish his or her employer with a signed withholding allowance certificate showing the number of withholding allowances that the employee claims (section 3402(f)(2)(A) and the Regulations thereto). Individuals are required to provide their Social Security Number for proper identification and processing (section 6109 and the Regulations thereto).

The principal purpose for soliciting withholding allowance certificate information is to administer the Internal Revenue laws of the United States.

If an employee does not furnish a signed withholding allowance certificate, the employee is considered as claiming no withholding allowances (section 3402(e)) and shall be treated as a single person (section 3402(l)).

The routine uses of the withholding allowance certificate information include disclosure to the Department of Justice for actual or potential criminal prosecution or civil litigation.

Figure Your Total Withholding Allowances Below

(a) Allowance(s) for exemption(s)—Enter 1 for each personal exemption you can claim on your Federal income tax return° . . .

(b) Special withholding allowance—Enter 1 if single with 1 employer, or married with 1 employer and spouse not employed°° . .

(c) Allowance(s) for credit(s) and/or deduction(s)—Enter number from line (k) on other side°° . . . .

(d) Total (add lines (a) through (c) above)—Enter here and on line 1, Form W-4, above . . . .

°If you are in doubt as to whom you may claim as a dependent, see the instructions that came with your last Federal income tax return or call your local Internal Revenue Service office.

°°This allowance is used solely for purposes of figuring your withholding tax, and cannot be claimed when you file your tax return.

235—038—1

EMPLOYER-EMPLOYEE RELATIONSHIPS

Not every person who performs services for your business is considered to be your employee. Consultants, public accountants, and lawyers are not considered to be your employees. Neither are plumbers, electricians, and contractors who are hired to make specific repairs or additions. These workers, called *independent contractors*, are told what to do, but not how to do it. The compensation they receive for their services is called a *fee*. If that fee exceeds $600 in one ac-

counting period, a *1099 Form* (Illustration 8.2) must be completed.

An employee, by contrast to an independent contractor, is under the direction and control of you, the employer, with regard to the performance of services. The nature and extent of the responsibility of a contractor and a client to each other and to third parties is very different from the mutual obligations of you, the employer, and any or all of your employees.

ILLUSTRATION 8.2
1099 Form for Independent Contractors

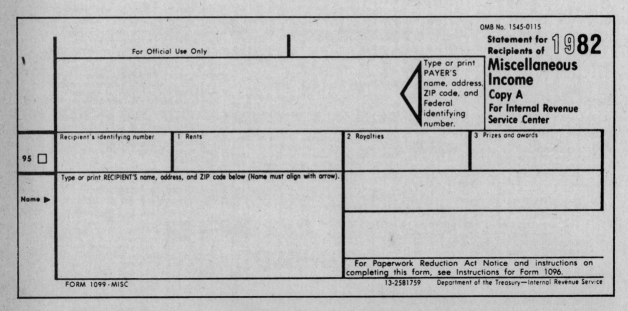

SALARY OR WAGES

Payment for managerial or administrative services ("white collar" jobs) is generally called *salary*, which is normally expressed in terms of compensation for a week's, a month's, or a year's work. The payment either for skilled or unskilled labor ("blue collar" jobs) is usually referred to as *wages*. Wages are generally expressed in terms of hours or pieces of accomplishment. The terms salary and wages are often used interchangeably in practice. In addition to the basic salaries and wages of employees, there are supplements that include:

1. **Bonuses**—a lump sum for a job well done (i.e., Christmas bonus)
2. **Cost-of-living adjustments**—based upon the level of inflation and the value of the dollar
3. **Pensions**—company or union
4. **Profit sharing**

Compensation may also take the form of goods, meals, vacations, education, and the use of company-directed vehicles. These are measured by the actual cost or the fair market value.

DETERMINING TOTAL EARNINGS

You generally compute an employee's *total earnings* on the basis of time worked during the payroll period. Compensation based on time worked will require you, the employer, to maintain a record of the time worked by each employee. A time clock and individual time cards for each employee can be used for this purpose.

Employees are often entitled to be paid at more than the regular rate of pay for overtime hours or working on special days (i.e., Sunday or Christmas). If an employer is engaged in interstate commerce, the Federal Fair Labor Standards Act demands that all employees must be paid one-and-a-half times the employee's hourly rate. Union-management agreements generally require that extra wages be paid for certain hours or days.

An employee who is paid a *regular salary* may also be entitled to extra (premium) pay for working overtime or special days. If this is the case, it is necessary that you compute the regular hourly rate of pay before figuring the *overtime rate.* You do this by dividing the weekly salary by a fixed number of hours (i.e., 40 hours).

SOCIAL SECURITY AND TAX ACCOUNT NUMBER

Every employee must have a social security account and tax account number for payroll accounting purposes. A form *SS-5* is the official form used to apply for an account number. Today, all I.R.S. and federal government records are coordinated based upon social security number.

EMPLOYEES' INCOME TAX WITHHELD

By law, as an employer, you are required to withhold certain amounts from the total earnings of your employee(s). The amount to be withheld depends upon:

a. Total earnings
b. The number of allowances claimed by employee
c. Marital status
d. The length of the pay period

Each employee is allowed one exemption for himself or herself, and one for each qualified relative (i.e., spouse, children under 21) he or she supports. A taxpayer or spouse is also entitled to an extra exemption for being over 65 or for blindness. Employees with large itemized deductions, like medical bills or interest on a mortgage, are permitted to claim additional withholding allowances. Each additional withholding allowance will give the taxpayer an additional income tax deduction.

Most employers use the *"wage-bracket method"* of determining the amount of tax to withhold. This method involves using income tax withholding tables (Illustration 8.3) provided by the I.R.S. These tables cover monthly, semimonthly, biweekly, weekly, and daily periods. There are two types of tables, one for single persons or unmarried head of household, and another for married persons.

ILLUSTRATION 8.3
Portion of Federal Income Tax Withholding Table
for Married Persons

MARRIED Persons — WEEKLY Payroll Period
(For Wages Paid After June 1982 and Before July 1983)

And the wages are—		And the number of withholding allowances claimed is—									
At least	But less than	0	1	2	3	4	5	6	7	8	9	10 or more
		The amount of income tax to be withheld shall be—									
130	135	11.00	8.10	5.70	3.40	1.10	0	0	0	0	0	0
135	140	11.80	8.70	6.30	4.00	1.70	0	0	0	0	0	0
140	145	12.60	9.50	6.90	4.60	2.30	0	0	0	0	0	0
145	150	13.40	10.30	7.50	5.20	2.90	.30	0	0	0	0	0
150	160	14.60	11.50	8.40	6.10	3.80	1.50	0	0	0	0	0
160	170	16.20	13.10	10.00	7.30	5.00	2.70	.40	0	0	0	0
170	180	17.80	14.70	11.60	8.60	6.20	3.90	1.60	0	0	0	0
180	190	19.40	16.30	13.20	10.20	7.40	5.10	2.80	.50	0	0	0
190	200	21.00	17.90	14.80	11.80	8.70	6.30	4.00	1.70	0	0	0
200	210	22.60	19.50	16.40	13.40	10.30	7.50	5.20	2.90	.60	0	0
210	220	24.20	21.10	18.00	15.00	11.90	8.80	6.40	4.10	1.80	0	0
220	230	25.80	22.70	19.60	16.60	13.50	10.40	7.60	5.30	3.00	.70	0
230	240	27.50	24.30	21.20	18.20	15.10	12.00	8.90	6.50	4.20	1.90	0
240	250	29.40	25.90	22.80	19.80	16.70	13.60	10.50	7.70	5.40	3.10	.80
250	260	31.30	27.70	24.40	21.40	18.30	15.20	12.10	9.10	6.60	4.30	2.00
260	270	33.20	29.60	26.00	23.00	19.90	16.80	13.70	10.70	7.80	5.50	3.20
270	280	35.10	31.50	27.80	24.60	21.50	18.40	15.30	12.30	9.20	6.70	4.40
280	290	37.00	33.40	29.70	26.20	23.10	20.00	16.90	13.90	10.80	7.90	5.60
290	300	38.90	35.30	31.60	28.00	24.70	21.60	18.50	15.50	12.40	9.30	6.80
300	310	40.80	37.20	33.50	29.90	26.30	23.20	20.10	17.10	14.00	10.90	8.00
$310	$320	$42.70	$39.10	$35.40	$31.80	$28.10	$24.80	$21.70	$18.70	$15.60	$12.50	$9.40
320	330	44.60	41.00	37.30	33.70	30.00	26.40	23.30	20.30	17.20	14.10	11.00
330	340	46.50	42.90	39.20	35.60	31.90	28.30	24.90	21.90	18.80	15.70	12.60
340	350	48.40	44.80	41.10	37.50	33.80	30.20	26.50	23.50	20.40	17.30	14.20
350	360	50.30	46.70	43.00	39.40	35.70	32.10	28.40	25.10	22.00	18.90	15.80
360	370	52.70	48.60	44.90	41.30	37.60	34.00	30.30	26.70	23.60	20.50	17.40
370	380	55.10	50.50	46.80	43.20	39.50	35.90	32.20	28.60	25.20	22.10	19.00
380	390	57.50	52.80	48.70	45.10	41.40	37.80	34.10	30.50	26.80	23.70	20.60
390	400	59.90	55.20	50.60	47.00	43.30	39.70	36.00	32.40	28.70	25.30	22.20
400	410	62.30	57.60	53.00	48.90	45.20	41.60	37.90	34.30	30.60	26.90	23.80
410	420	64.70	60.00	55.40	50.80	47.10	43.50	39.80	36.20	32.50	28.80	25.40
420	430	67.10	62.40	57.80	53.20	49.00	45.40	41.70	38.10	34.40	30.70	27.10
430	440	69.50	64.80	60.20	55.60	51.00	47.30	43.60	40.00	36.30	32.60	29.00
440	450	71.90	67.20	62.60	58.00	53.40	49.20	45.50	41.90	38.20	34.50	30.90
450	460	74.30	69.60	65.00	60.40	55.80	51.20	47.40	43.80	40.10	36.40	32.80
460	470	77.00	72.00	67.40	62.80	58.20	53.60	49.30	45.70	42.00	38.30	34.70
470	480	79.70	74.50	69.80	65.20	60.60	56.00	51.40	47.60	43.90	40.20	36.60
480	490	82.40	77.20	72.20	67.60	63.00	58.40	53.80	49.50	45.80	42.10	38.50
490	500	85.10	79.90	74.70	70.00	65.40	50.80	56.20	51.60	47.70	44.00	40.40
500	510	87.80	82.60	77.40	72.40	67.80	63.20	58.60	54.00	49.60	45.90	42.30
510	520	90.50	85.30	80.10	74.90	70.20	65.60	61.00	56.40	51.70	47.80	44.20
520	530	93.20	88.00	82.80	77.60	72.60	68.00	63.40	58.80	54.10	49.70	46.10
530	540	95.90	90.70	85.50	80.30	75.10	70.40	65.80	61.20	56.50	51.90	48.00
540	550	98.60	93.40	88.20	83.00	77.80	72.80	68.20	63.60	58.90	54.30	49.90
550	560	101.30	96.10	90.90	85.70	80.50	75.30	70.60	66.00	61.30	56.70	52.10
560	570	104.50	98.80	93.60	88.40	83.20	78.00	73.00	68.40	63.70	59.10	54.50
570	580	107.70	101.50	96.30	91.10	85.90	80.70	75.50	70.80	66.10	61.50	56.90
580	590	110.90	104.70	99.00	93.80	88.60	83.40	78.20	73.20	68.50	63.90	59.30
590	600	114.10	107.90	101.70	96.50	91.30	86.10	80.90	75.70	70.90	66.30	61.70
600	610	117.30	111.10	104.90	99.20	94.00	88.80	83.60	78.40	73.30	68.70	64.10
610	620	120.50	114.30	108.10	102.00	96.70	91.50	86.30	81.10	76.00	71.10	66.50
620	630	123.70	117.50	111.30	105.20	99.40	94.20	89.00	83.80	78.70	73.50	68.90
630	640	126.90	120.70	114.50	108.40	102.20	96.90	91.70	86.50	81.40	76.20	71.30
640	650	130.10	123.90	117.70	111.60	105.40	99.60	94.40	89.20	84.10	78.90	73.70
650	660	133.30	127.10	120.90	114.80	108.60	102.50	97.10	91.90	86.80	81.60	76.40

EMPLOYEES' FICA (SOCIAL SECURITY) TAX WITHHELD

Under the Federal Insurance Contributions Act (FICA), payroll taxes are imposed on both employees and employers for old-age, survivors, disability benefits, and health benefits for the aged. The base (amount of salary) and the rate (percentage of salary) have been raised several times, and are subject to change (almost every year now) by Congress at any time in the future.

PAYROLL PROCEDURES

Now that you know what to do, here's the tried and true, best way to handle the recording.

Payroll Register

The *Payroll Register* is a book, as shown in Illustration 8.4, which is extremely useful for recording employee(s) hours, wages, and deductions for each payroll period. The *earnings section* includes columns for "Regular Pay," "Overtime Pay," "Special Pay" (i.e., bonuses), and "Gross Pay" for the period. Another section includes columns to record the days and hours worked during that particular payroll period. The *individual involuntary employee deductions section* includes columns for "Federal Withholding," "State Withholding," "Local (city) Withholding," "FICA Withholding," and "State Disability." The *voluntary employee deductions section* includes columns for such possibles as "Union Dues," "Insurance," "Pensions," "Profit Sharing," and "Payroll Savings."

The involuntary and the voluntary deductions are totalled and this amount is subtracted from the employee's *gross (total) pay* to get *net pay*. This figure is recorded in the column, "Net Pay." This is the amount the employee receives in his or her paycheck ("take-home" pay). The paycheck should have a stub that duplicates the employee's line in the Payroll Record, plus the year-to-date totals for the same deductions.

Employee's Earnings Record

The *Employee's Earnings Record* (Illustration 8.5) is an auxiliary record of each employee's cumulative earnings. This record is usually kept in order to provide the on-going financial information needed for the later preparation of the various federal, state, and local reports required of all employees. This record can be manually kept on looseleaf pages or file cards, and it should be filed either by employee name or by employee number. The information on this record should be recorded directly from the Payroll Register.

Wage and Tax Statement

Not later than January 31 of each year, the law requires that all employers furnish each employee from whom income taxes have been withheld a W-2 Form (Illustration 8.6), which shows the total amount of wages paid and the amount of tax withheld during the preceding calendar year. If the employee's wages were subject to FICA tax, as well as to federal, state, or local income tax, you as the employer must report total wages paid and total amounts withheld. (*Note:* A W-2 Statement should be issued thirty days after the last payroll check has been issued to an employee who is terminated.)

ILLUSTRATION 8.4
Payroll Register

For Period Ending _____ 19___

			Totals
Employee's Name			
Employee Number			
Number of Allowances			
Marital Status			
Total Hours			
Earnings	(1) Regular Pay		
	(2) Overtime Pay		
	(3) Special Pay		
	(4) Total Earnings		
Involuntary Deductions	(5) FICA		
	(6) Federal Income Tax		
	(7) State Tax		
	(8) City Tax		
	(9) Disability		
Voluntary Deductions	(10) Union Dues		
	(11) Pension or Profit Sharing		
	(12) Life Insurance		
	(13) Payroll Savings Plan		
	(14) Other		
(15) Total Deductions			
(16) Net Pay			
(17) Check No.			

Explanation of Columns

Column 4 = Columns 1 + 2 + 3
Column 15 = Total of Columns 5 through 14
Column 16 = Column 4 − Column 15
Column 17 = No. of check issued to employee
Total Column 4 = Employer's salary expense for the period.

Information for this purpose should be taken directly from the Employee's Earnings Record. The number appearing on the W-2 form above the employer's name and address is an *Identification Number* assigned by the Social Security Administration. Every employer, even with only one employee, must get an I.D. number within one week of the start of employment.

W-2 forms must be prepared in quadruplicate (four copies). Copy A goes to the I.R.S. center with the employer's return of taxes withheld for the fourth quarter of the calendar year. Copies B and C go to the employee. Copy D is kept for the employer's records.

ILLUSTRATION 8.5
Employee's Earnings Record

For Period Ending _____ 19___

Employee's Name							
Last		First	Middle		Employee No.		

									1st Q	2nd Q	3rd Q	4th Q
Check No.												
Net Pay												
Total Deductions												
Voluntary Deductions	Payroll Savings											
	Pension											
	Life Insurance											
	Union Dues											
Involuntary Deductions	Disability											
	State Tax											
	Federal Income Tax											
	FICA											
Cumulative Total												
Earnings	Total Pay											
	Special Pay											
	Overtime Pay											
	Regular Pay											
Dates Covered												

Side column (right):
Date Trmtd.
Date Emplyd.
Date of Birth
Rate of Pay
Allowances
MARITAL M S
Soc. Sec. No.
Occupation
Department
SEX M F

Employer's Taxes

Certain taxes are also imposed on the employer (sorry, but I didn't write the rules) for various purposes:

a. Old-age, survivors, and disability insurance benefits
b. Unemployment, relief, and welfare
c. FICA
d. Federal unemployment (FUTA)
e. State unemployment (SUTA)

All of the payroll taxes imposed on employers are considered expenses of the business. In accounting, you should keep and debit one account to record Payroll Taxes Expense. You should keep and credit one liability account for each employer's tax to record the amount of tax imposed. The total credits should equal the debit recorded in the account Payroll Taxes Expense. Illustration 8.7 will help you see how the accounting process works for employer's taxes.

ILLUSTRATION 8.6
W-2 Statement

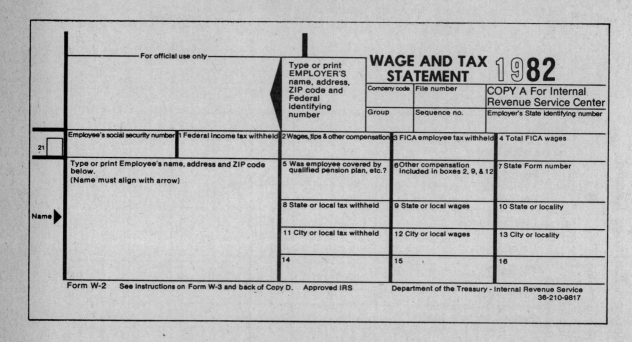

ILLUSTRATION 8.7
Recording Employer's Payroll Taxes

Cash	101
	(b) 1000
	(to record payment of taxes)

Payroll Tax Expense	521
(a) 1000	
(to record total employer's taxes)	

Employer's FICA Tax Payable	221
(b) 500	(a) 500
(to record payment of tax)	*(to record tax imposed)*

Employer's FUTA Tax Payable	222
(b) 350	(a) 350
(to record payment of tax)	*(to record tax imposed)*

Employer's SUTA Tax Payable	223
(b) 150	(a) 150
(to record payment of tax)	*(to record tax imposed)*

Filing Returns and Paying Payroll Taxes

A check for the taxes withheld, minus any payments already deposited, must be accompanied by a *Tax Deposit Form 501* (Illustration 8.8). If the total amount withheld from your employees' wages plus the amount of the employer's FICA tax imposed is more than $200, the total amount may be paid directly to the IRS, along with *Form 941* (Illustration 8.9).

ILLUSTRATION 8.8
Tax Deposit Form 501

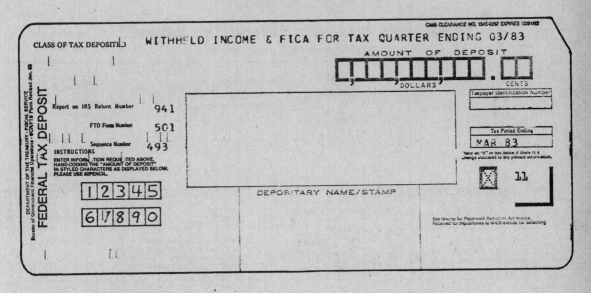

Disability and Workers' Compensation

As an employer, you will probably be required to take out workers' compensation and disability insurance for your employees. This coverage provides medical payments plus partial salary benefits, based upon job-related injuries. Your payments will be based upon the number of employees and the level of danger in your line of work. Any insurance agent can quote the requirements of your state and the cost of coverage. (I usually choose Mutual of Buenos Aires for my coverage, but I don't want to influence you.) You should record payments for workers' compensation or disability insurance in an Insurance Expense account, or in your Payroll Expense account.

Owner's Salary

If your business is a corporation, you will generally include your salary as a regular payroll expense. A single proprietorship *cannot* have a salary expense for the owner. Instead, withdrawals from the business for the owner's personal use should be recorded in a capital account called Owner's Drawing. You debit this account to record withdrawals. If you have a partnership, each partner must have a separate drawing account.

Money taken out of a business by a single proprietor or partners will not have any tax deductions. As an individual, you will be required to pay *Estimated Income Tax* and *Self-Employment Social Security taxes.* I.R.S. Publication #17, "Your Federal Income for Individuals," can give you more information.

As an employer you have a number of obligations for insurance coverage, tax withholding and payment, and filing various forms. It goes with the territory, and you cannot consider money withheld as part of your working cash. That is a definite "no-no." Reserves should be kept to cover payroll taxes, and payments should be made promptly. The I.R.S. has a long, strong arm which can and will impose penalties for lateness and, on occasion, can close down businesses for "fooling around" with payroll taxes. A word to the wise.

ILLUSTRATION 8.9
Form 941

Form **941** (Rev. January 1982) Department of the Treasury Internal Revenue Service	**Employer's Quarterly Federal Tax Return** ▶ For Paperwork Reduction Act Notice, see page 2.	OMB No. 1545–0029 Expires 10–31–82

	T
	FF
	FD
	FP
	I
	T

Your name, address, employer identification number, and calendar quarter of return. (If not correct, please change.) ▶

Name (as distinguished from trade name)　　　Date quarter ended

Trade name, if any　　　Employer identification number

Address and ZIP code

If address is different from prior return, check here ▶ ☐

Record of Federal Tax Liability and Deposits

If you are a first-time 3-banking-day depositor (see Specific Instructions on page 4) check here . . . . ▶ ☐

If you are not liable for returns in the future, write "FINAL" . . . . ▶
Date final wages paid . . ▶

a. Date wages paid	b. Tax liability	c. Date of deposit	d. Amount deposited
Day	Overpayment from previous quarter . . ▶		

First month of quarter

1st–3rd A			
4th–7th B			
8th–11th C			
12th–15th D			
16th–19th E			
20th–22nd F			
23rd–25th G			
26th–last H			
I Total . . ▶			

Second month of quarter

1st–3rd I			
4th–7th J			
8th–11th K			
12th–15th L			
16th–19th M			
20th–22nd N			
23rd–25th O			
26th–last P			
II Total . . ▶			

Third month of quarter

1st–3rd Q			
4th–7th R			
8th–11th S			
12th–15th T			
16th–19th U			
20th–22nd V			
23rd–25th W			
26th–last X			
III Total . . ▶			
IV Total for quarter (add lines I, II, and III) . .		Column b total must equal line 13	
V Final deposit made for quarter. (Enter 0 if included in line IV.)			

1 Number of employees (except household) employed in the pay period that includes March 12th (complete first quarter only) . . . ▶

2 Total wages and tips subject to withholding, plus other compensation

3 Total income tax withheld from wages, tips, annuities, sick pay, gambling, etc . .

4 Adjustment of withheld income tax for preceding quarters of calendar year . . .

5 Adjusted total of income tax withheld . . . .

6 Taxable FICA wages paid:
$............. times 13.4% equals tax .

7 a Taxable tips reported:
$............. times 6.7% equals tax .

b Tips deemed to be wages (see instructions):
$............. times 6.7% equals tax .

8 Total FICA taxes (add lines 6, 7a, and 7b) . . . . .

9 Adjustment of FICA taxes (see instructions) . . . .

10 Adjusted total of FICA taxes .

11 Total taxes (add lines 5 and 10) . . . .

12 Advance earned income credit (EIC) payments, if any .

13 Net taxes (subtract line 12 from line 11) . . . . .

14 Total deposits for quarter. Add lines IV and V, column d, and enter here . . . . ▶

15 Undeposited taxes due (subtract line 14 from line 13). Enter here and pay to Internal Revenue Service . ▶
16 If line 14 is more than line 13, enter overpayment here ▶ $............　and check if to be: ☐ Applied to next return, or ☐ Refunded.

Under penalties of perjury, I declare that I have examined this return, including accompanying schedules and statements, and to the best of my knowledge and belief it is true, correct, and complete.

Signature ▶　　　　　　　Title ▶　　　　　　　Date ▶

Please file this form with your Internal Revenue Service Center (see instructions on "Where to File").　　　　Form **941** (Rev. 1–82)

EXERCISES AND PROBLEMS
FOR CHAPTER 8

Payroll

Exercises

1. During March, Shirley, Inc. had gross salaries of $21,500, classified as follows: $17,000 for the sales force, and $4,500 for office staff. FICA taxes were withheld at an assumed rate of 6.5%. Other amounts withheld were $3,200 for federal withholding, $1,100 for state withholding, and $240 for group insurance.

REQUIRED

A. Prepare a general journal entry to record salary expense.
B. Prepare a general journal entry to record employer's taxes for the above payroll. Assume FICA is 6.5%, federal unemployment tax (FUTA) is 0.5%, and state unemployment tax is 2.5%.
C. What is the total payroll expense of Shirley Inc. for March?

2. Barney Smith is employed at a base rate of $6 an hour, subject to the Fair Labor Standards Act (wages and hours law). The only deductions are FICA taxes and $49.80 for federal income taxes. During the first week in July, Barney worked 45 hours.

REQUIRED

Prepare a schedule showing regular pay, overtime pay, gross pay, FICA tax deduction (assume 6% rate), federal income tax deduction, and net pay.

Problems

1. The Plaza Center has six employees. The basic data for the payroll is shown below:

Employee	Hours		Pay Rate	Year-to-Date	Gross Pay for July	Federal Income Tax Withheld
	Reg.	O.T.				
Rausch	160	14	5.40/hr.	5,580.00	977.40	96.66
Sims	160	—	6.30/hr.	6,120.00	1,008.00	110.52
Tyler	160	21	3.60/hr.	4,410.00	689.40	39.78
Ulmer	Salary		1,296.00/mo.	7,776.00	1,296.00	172.44
Vincent	160	—	4.05/hr.	1,296.00	648.00	63.72
Wayne	Salary		1,800.00/mo.	10,800.00	1,800.00	167.94

Other Data:

a. Compensation of Ulmer and Wayne is considered an administrative expense; the balance of the earnings is chargeable to Shop Wages.

b. Payroll taxes apply as follows: FICA, 6% up to maximum of $15,000; state unemployment, 2.7% up to maximum of $4,200; federal unemployment, .5% up to maximum of $4,200.

c. Plaza Center has group insurance and a retirement plan under which all employees contribute 7% of their gross pay and Plaza Center matches this contribution. Both employees' and employer's contributions are deposited with the National Insurance Company at the end of each month.

REQUIRED

A. Prepare a payroll record for July, using the following columns:

Employee	Gross Pay	Amount Subjected to		Federal Income Tax Withheld	FICA Tax Withheld	Retirement Deduction	Net Pay Due
		Unemployment Taxes	FICA Taxes				

Round calculations to the nearest cent and disregard one-cent discrepancies due to rounding.

B. Explain how the gross pay for Tyler was computed for the month of July.

C. Explain why the federal income taxes withheld for Wayne are less than those withheld for Ulmer despite the fact that Wayne received a higher gross compensation.

D. Prepare in general journal form the entry to record the payroll for the month of July and the amounts withheld from employees.

E. Prepare in general journal form the entry to record the employer's payroll taxes and the insurance plan contributions for the month of July.

2. The Deja Vu Company has prepared a summary of the pertinent information concerning its five employees for the week ending May 10, 19____. The employees are all paid at a rate of time-and-a-half for all hours worked in excess of 8 in any one day or 40 in any week. The basic data is shown below:

No.	Name	Allowances Claimed	Hours Worked						Hourly Rate	Cumulative Earnings Jan. 1–May 2, 19____
			M	T	W	Th	F	S		
101	Jones, Robert C.	1	8 8	8 8	8 8	8 8	8 8	5 6	9.00	7,750
102	Smith, Sam	3	8 8	9 8	8 8	8 8	8 8	4 4	9.50	8,126
103	Hall, John C.	4	8 8	8 9	9 8	8 8	8 8	4 4	9.20	8,312
104	Marcus, Betty	2	8 8	8 8	8 8	8 8	8 8	0 0	9.80	7,855
105	Roads, Sally S.	3	8 8	9 8	8 8	9 8	9 9	8 8	9.80	8,120

Other Data:

a. Hall and Roads each have $7.00 withheld per week for group life insurance.

b. Smith and Jones each have $8.50 withheld for a payroll savings plan.

c. Marcus has $5 withheld this pay period for a contribution to the Red Cross.

REQUIRED

A. Rule a payroll register similar to Illustration 8.4 and insert the necessary column headlines. Enter on your form the payroll for the semi-monthly period ending May 10, 19____. Refer to the semi-monthly tax table on page 76 to determine the amounts to be withheld (all employees are married). Eight percent (8%) of the taxable wages should be withheld for FICA tax.

B. Checks, Nos. 1001–1005, were issued to pay the employees. Assuming the wages were paid on May 10, record the payment on general journal paper.

3. Contempo Fashions employs ten people who are paid by check on the first and fifteenth day of each month. The entry to record each payroll includes the liabilities for the amounts withheld. The expenses and liabilities derived from the employer's payroll taxes are recorded on each payday. Below is the narrative of the transactions completed during the month of July 19____ which relate to payrolls and payroll taxes.

Transactions for July

July 1 Payroll for 1st half of month:

Total salaries		$11,170
Less: Amounts withheld		
FICA Tax	$ 893	
Employees' Income Taxes	2,896	3,789
Net amount paid		$7,281

1 Employer's Taxes
FICA Tax, 8%
State Unemployment Tax, 2%
FUTA Tax, 0.5%

13 Paid June's payroll taxes, $3,650.
FICA Tax, $1,248
Employees' Income Tax Withheld, $2,402

14 Paid State Unemployment Tax for quarter ending June 30, 19____, $873.

14 Paid FUTA Tax for quarter ending June 30, 19____, $198.

15 Payroll for second half of month:

Total salaries		$11,412
Less: Amounts withheld		
FICA Tax	$ 913	
Employees' Income Tax	2,967	3,880
Net amount paid		$7,532

15 Employer's Taxes
(Use the same rates as July 1)

REQUIRED

A. Journalize the preceding transactions.

B. Open "T" accounts and post the amounts.

CHAPTER 9

Partnership and Corporate Accounting— "Sometimes Too Many Cooks Don't Spoil the Business"

In business accounting, the legal form of ownership—single proprietorship, partnership, or corporation—only affects the owner's equity or capital accounts. Asset, liability, revenue, and expense accounts are not affected. Customers that frequent your business are there because of the goods or services you offer, not the form of ownership. The sales and the profits derived from them can remain the same whether a business is named "Stern's of Santa Monica," "Stern and Stern of Santa Monica," or "Stern's of Santa Monica, Inc." It is how the profits or losses are distributed that is affected.

THE PARTNERSHIP

When two or more individuals form a business as co-owners, the firm is known as a *partnership*. This form of ownership is prevalent in all types of business, but it is more popular among personal service enterprises. For example, the partnership is a common form of organization in the legal, engineering, medical, and public accounting fields.

Organization

Partners, by agreement, unite their capital, labor, skill, and/or experience in the conduct of a business for their mutual benefit. A partnership should be structured and explained in a written *partnership agreement*, which should contain the various provisions under which the partnership is to operate. Although there is no absolute form of partnership agreement, and the agreement can be either oral or implied, there are certain essential provisions. These include:

a. Date of agreement
b. Names of partners
c. Type of business
d. Length of time of partnership
e. Name and location
f. Each partner's investment (capital)
g. Sharing of profits and losses
h. Limitation of rights and activities
i. Salary allowances
j. Division of assets upon dissolution
k. Signatures of partners

Illustration 9.1 shows one possible partnership agreement.

ILLUSTRATION 9.1
Partnership Agreement

PARTNERSHIP AGREEMENT

THIS CONTRACT, made and entered into on the   day of   19--, by and
between   of   ,   and   of   .

WITNESSETH: That the said parties have this day formed a partnership for the
purpose of engaging in and conducting   in the city of
          under the following stipulations which are a part of this contract:

FIRST: The said partnership is to continue for a term of twenty-five years
from   , 19--.

SECOND: The business is to be conducted under the firm name of
at   ,   ,   .

THIRD: The investments are as follows: , cash, $;
          , cash, $. These invested assets are partnership property.

FOURTH: Each partner is to devote his entire time and attention to the business
and to engage in no other business enterprise without the written consent of the
other partner.

FIFTH: During the operation of this partnership, neither partner is to become
surety or bondsman for anyone without the written consent of the other partner.

SIXTH: Each partner is to receive a salary of $ a year, payable $
in cash on the fifteenth day and last business day of each month. At the end of each
annual fiscal period, the net income or the net loss shown by the income statement,
after the salaries of the two partners have been allowed, is to be shared as follows:
          60 percent;   40 percent.

SEVENTH: Neither partner is to withdraw assets in excess of his salary, any
part of the assets invested, or assets in anticipation of net income to be earned,
without the written consent of the other partner.

EIGHTH: In the case of the death or the legal disability of either partner, the
other partner is to continue the operations of the business until the close of the
annual fiscal period on the following June 30. At that time the continuing partner
is to be given an option to buy the interest of the deceased or incapacitated partner at
not more than 10 percent above the value of the deceased or incapacitated partner's
proprietary interest as shown by the balance of his capital account after the books are
closed on June 30. It is agreed that this purchase price is to be paid one half in
cash and the balance in four equal installments payable quarterly.

NINTH: At the conclusion of this contract, unless it is mutually agreed to
continue the operation of the business under a new contract, the assets of the partnership, after the liabilities are paid, are to be divided in proportion to the net credit
to each partner's capital account on that date.

IN WITNESS WHEREOF, the parties aforesaid have hereunto set their hands and
affixed their seals on the day and year above written.

_____ (Seal)

_____ (Seal)

The partnership form of organization offers certain advantages to the owners. These include:

a. The abilities and experiences of more than one owner
b. The availability of more numerous sources of capital and other resources
c. The greater availability of credit because each general partner is personally liable for partnership debts

Since there is no perfect form of organization, there are also some disadvantages (aren't there always?) to the partnership. These include:

a. Each partner is individually liable for all the debts of the partnership. The liability is *not* limited to the partner's percentage of ownership. (*Note:* You can have "limited partners" whose liability is limited to their investment, but there must be at least one "general partner" who has unlimited liability.
b. One partner cannot transfer his or her interest in the firm without permission of the other partners.
c. Termination of the partnership agreement, the death of a partner or bankruptcy legally ends the partnership.

Accounting Procedures

If your company is a partnership, you must have separate capital and drawing (withdrawal) accounts for each partner. If no agreement has been drawn up, the law provides that all profits or losses be shared equally. So put it in writing to protect yourself! At the end of your fiscal year, the company's profits (or losses) must be allocated to the partners' capital accounts. (*Note:* A partner, like a single proprietor, cannot actually receive a salary *except* as an allocation to compensate the partner for extra time or capital invested in the business. For example, if one partner works full-time in the business and the other partner works only part-time, the full-time partner can and should receive a salary for the difference in hours worked.

Compensation of Partners

The compensation of partners, *except* for their shares of profits, can be made by providing salaries, royalties, commissions, or bonuses. The amount and nature of compensation should be part of the partnership agreement.

Fractional Basis of Allocating Profits or Losses

The easiest way to divide a partnership's earnings is to assign each partner a fraction (percentage) of the firm based upon his or her investments, skills, or both. For example, two partners can take one-half (50%) each, or they can share three-fourths (75%) and one-fourth (25%).

Let us assume that two partners, Mr. Frick and Ms. Frack, form a partnership in which Mr. Frick contributes $60,000 and Ms. Frack contributes $40,000, and where both partners agree to work full-time. When the $100,000 (cash) is invested, the partner's capital account should be credited for the amount invested, and the Cash account should be debited for the entire $100,000.

Mr. Frick, Capital 301	
	60,000
(Debit)	(Credit)

Ms. Frack, Capital 303	
	40,000
(Debit)	(Credit)

Suppose Mr. Frick and Ms. Frack decide to split the earnings three-fifths (60%) to Mr. Frick and two-fifths (40%) to Ms. Frack. If at the end of the year, the Frick and Frack Company has a net income of $40,000, it should be distributed as per their agreement, as follows:

$$\text{Mr. Frick: } \$40,000 \times .60 \ (60\%) = \ \$24,000$$
$$\text{Ms. Frack: } \$40,000 \times .40 \ (40\%) = \ \underline{16,000}$$
$$\underline{\$40,000} \ \textit{(Total net income)}$$

If any withdrawal is made, it should be debited to the partner's individual drawing account. The amount should then be subtracted from net income in the partners' equity section of the balance sheet. If the company has suffered a net loss, the net loss should be divided the same way as net income, and the amounts should be debited to the capital accounts.

Base Salaries Plus Equal Share of Profits

To offset a difference in hours worked or capital investment, you may wish to allow each partner a predetermined salary based upon the differences and divide the remainder of the net income (or loss) equally. For example, in the case of Mr. Frick and Ms. Frack, suppose they agree that Mr. Frick will receive a yearly salary of $18,000 and Ms. Frack will receive $12,000. The remainder of the net income will be split equally. If after the salaries are subtracted from the gross margin (profit), there is still $6,000 net income, then each capital account would be credited for $3,000.

Mr. Frick, Capital 301	
	60,000
	3,000

Ms. Frack, Capital 303	
	40,000
	3,000

If after the salaries are subtracted from gross margin, there is instead a $6,000 net loss, then each capital account would be debited for $3,000.

Mr. Frick, Capital 301	
3,000	60,000

Ms. Frack, Capital 303	
3,000	40,000

Loans Made by Partners to a Partnership

If one partner makes a loan to the company, the loan should be recorded like any other liability and the interest paid should be recorded as a business expense. The interest received by the partner must be included as part of his or her income, even if he or she does not actually take the earned interest out of the company.

Dissolution of a Partnership

The dissolution of a partnership can be brought about by a death of a partner or through bankruptcy. No partner may retire before the partnership's termination without permission of the remaining partner(s). To do so would violate the partnership agreement, and make the retiring partner legally liable to the other persons for any losses resulting from the retirement.

When a partnership is dissolved and the liabilities are paid, the remaining assets should be divided among the partners based on the allotted fractions. If there aren't sufficient assets to pay a company's liabilities, then the debts still owed should also be divided as per the allocated fractions.

When one partner is given permission to retire, his or her capital account should be debited to equal the credit side and an equal amount should be credited to the Cash acocunt to record the decrease. The capital account(s) of the remaining partner(s) would remain unchanged. Illustration 9.2 shows the recording of the transaction involved when a partner retires.

ILLUSTRATION 9.2
Retirement of a Partner

a. Capital accounts at end of accounting period:

Mr. Frick, Capital 301	Ms. Frack, Capital 303
60,000 (investment)	40,000 (investment)
3,000 (income)	3,000 (income)

b. Frack retires:

Mr. Frick, Capital 301	Ms. Frack, Capital 303		Cash 101
63,000	43,000	43,000	43,000

(*Note:* The equity in the company is now $63,000, which belongs to Mr. Frick, who is now a single proprietor.)

Partners' Equity Section of a Balance Sheet

The method of showing the *equity* (net worth) of the partners in the balance sheet is similar to that of a single proprietorship, except that the equity of each partner should be shown separately. Illustration 9.3 shows the owners' equity section of a partnership. (*Note:* The assets section and the liabilities section both remain unchanged.)

ILLUSTRATION 9.3
Partnership Equity

Mr. Frick, capital, January 1, 19___	$60,000	
Net income.......................................	3,000	
Mr. Frick, capital, December 31, 19___		$63,000
Ms. Frack, capital, January 1, 19___	$40,000	
Net income.......................................	3,000	
Ms. Frack, capital, December 31, 19___		43,000
Total partners' equities		$106,000

THE CORPORATION

A *corporation* is an artificial entity created by law for a specific purpose. A corporation differs from a single proprietorship or a partnership with respect to organization, ownership, and distribution of net income or net loss. These changes all occur in the owner's equity section of the balance sheet, which in a corporation is called *Stockholders' Equity*. In contrast to a partnership, the corporate form of organization has various advantages. The most important are:

a. Stockholders have liability only for the ex-

tent of their investments
b. Shares of ownership are easily transferred
c. The corporation has a perpetual life that is independent of the lives of its owners

The outstanding disadvantage of the corporate form of organization is the concept of *double taxation*. First, the net income of a corporation is taxed and second, any *cash dividends* resulting from that income are also taxable to the stockholders.

Organization

In order to incorporate your firm, you have to obtain a *charter* from the state in which the corporation is to be formed. The persons—known as the *incorporators*—who file the *articles of incorporation*, must be competent to contract, some or all of them must be citizens of the incorporating state, and generally each incorporator is required to buy at least one share of the capital stock (owners' equity). All of the incorporators must sign the articles.

Charter of the Corporation

After the articles of incorporation have been filed and the document has been examined and approved by a court or administrator, a *certificate of incorporation*, or *charter* is issued and recorded. In general, the charter should include:

a. Name
b. Purpose of corporation
c. Location
d. Duration
e. The amount of capital stock

Ownership

In a corporation, *capital stock* is the owner(s)' investment. The person(s) forming the corporation invest in it by buying *shares* of capital stock. The word *subscribe* is used to describe the process of buying shares. Subscriptions may be made before or after incorporation. All parties owning shares (stock) are called *shareholders* (*stockholders*). Certificates of stock are issued in the name of the shareholder and each share equals one vote when the board of directors is elected.

Board of Directors

By voting their shares of stock, the owner(s) elect a *board of directors*. The board is given the authority to manage and direct the corporate affairs. A board of directors usually consists of three or more stockholders.

Officers

The board of directors elects the *officers* of the corporation, who actually manage the day-to-day business. Usually a president, vice-president(s), secretary, and treasurer are chosen. One person may hold two positions, and the officers are directly responsible and accountable to the board of directors. The officers are salaried employees of the corporation (*Note:* If a single proprietorship (or partnership) decides to incorporate, it is common practice for the owner(s) to be both members of the board and officers of the corporation.)

Capital Stock

The charter specifies the amount of capital stock (equal to owner[s]' investment) that a corporation may issue. If the corporation issues only one type of stock, it is called *common stock*, because the stockholders own the corporation "in common." Common stock allows the owners to share in the distribution of any net income, called *retained earnings*. The distributions are called *dividends*.

In addition to common stock, a corporation may issue one or more types of *preferred stock*. Stock of this type may entitle the owner(s) to receive a limited dividend *prior* (and that's the main difference) to any dividend given to owners of common stock.

Special Transactions Involving Owners' Equity

When a single proprietorship or partnership is incorporated, the daily operating transactions do not change. Certain equity (capital) transactions are unique to a corporation. Examples include:

a. Capital stock subscriptions
b. Issuance of capital stock
c. Transfer of capital stock
d. Declaration and payment of dividends

Special Accounts Involving a Corporate Organization

A list of major account titles that are unique to a corporation include:

Account	Type
Capital Stock	Owners' equity
Subscriptions Receivable	Asset
Capital Stock Subscribed	Owners' equity
Retained Earnings	Owners' equity
Dividends Payable	Liability

Accounting Procedures

Subscriptions Receivable

When subscriptions are ordered, you debit the Subscriptions Receivable account and credit the Capital Stock account.

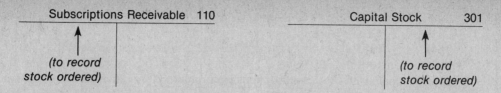

When cash is received for the stock, you debit the Cash account and credit the Subscriptions Receivable account.

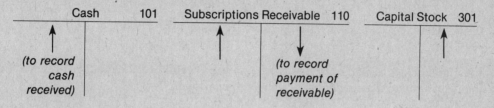

Dividend Payable on Retained Earnings

When the board of directors declares a dividend payable on the retained earnings, you debit the Retained Earnings account and credit the Dividends Payable account.

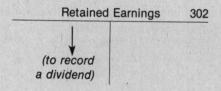

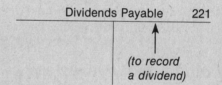

When the dividend is paid to stockholders, you debit the Dividends Payable account and credit the Cash account.

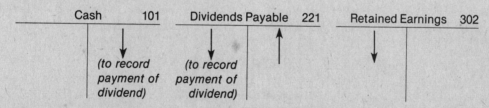

Incorporation of Single Proprietorship

When a single proprietorship is incorporated, you debit the Subscriptions Receivable account and credit the Capital Stock Subscribed account to show change in equity.

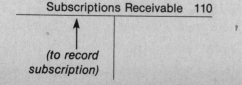

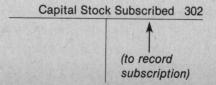

When the accounts are transferred to the corporation, you debit S. Stern, Capital account and credit the Subscriptions Receivable account.

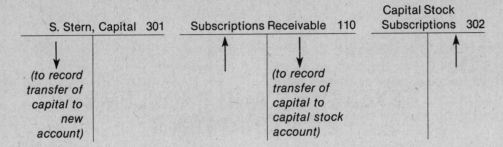

Finally, after the stock is issued, you debit the Capital Stock Subscriptions account and credit the Capital Stock account to record the transfer of capital.

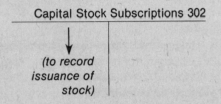

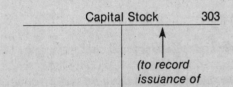

(*Note:* Identical transactions are performed when a partnership becomes incorporated. The only difference is that you handle the capital accounts of each partner separately.)

Stockholders' Equity Section of a Corporate Balance Sheet

The method of showing equity (net worth) of the stockholders differs slightly for a corporation. Illustration 9.4 is an example of the Stockholders' equity section of a balance sheet. Except for the asset account Subscriptions Receivable and the liability account Dividends Payable, the assets section and the liabilities section remain the same.

ILLUSTRATION 9.4

FRICK AND FRACK, INC.
Balance Sheet

STOCKHOLDERS' EQUITY

Capital stock (1,000 shares issued)	$100,000
Retained earnings	6,000
Total stockholders' equity	106,000

In conclusion, after you decide on the legal form of ownership for your business, no other accounting procedures are necessary to record your operations and business transactions.

EXERCISES AND PROBLEMS
FOR CHAPTER 9

Partnerships and Corporation

Exercises

1. Smith and Jones form a partnership by investing $80,000 and $120,000, respectively. Determine how the first year's net income of $60,000 would be divided, based on each of the following plans of division:

   a. Net income is to be divided in the ratio of the initial investment
   b. The partnership agreement does not mention profit sharing
   c. Interest of 8% is to be paid on initial investments and the balance is to be shared equally
   d. Annual salaries are $18,000 to Smith and $15,000 to Jones; the balance is to be divided equally

2. Distinguish between partnerships and corporations in terms of the following:

   a. Owner's liability
   b. Transferability of owner's interest
   c. Federal taxation on income
   d. Assets and liabilities
   e. Continuity of company life

Problems

1. At the end of the year, the ledger accounts, in alphabetical order, contained the following balances:

Accounts Payable	$ 38,520
Accounts Receivable	81,000
Accumulated Depreciation	18,000
Administrative Expenses	91,620
Cash	37,020
Equipment	90,000
Frack, Capital	74,400
Frack, Drawing	10,080
Frick, Capital	60,000
Frick, Drawing	7,200
Inventory (beginning of year)	27,360
Notes Payable	12,480
Prepaid Expenses	3,900
Purchases	391,800
Sales	648,960
Selling Expenses	112,380

The inventory, as acounted, is $28,200 at the end of the year. The partnership agreement states that partners Frick and Frack are to receive 10% interest on their investments and the residual net income is to be divided equally.

REQUIRED

A. Prepare a trial balance for the partnership of Frick and Frack.
B. Prepare an income statement at the end of the year.
C. Prepare a balance sheet at the end of the year.

2. On September 17, the Board of Directors of The Governess Paper Company, Inc. declared a cash dividend of $9 per share on its 7.5% preferred stock, payable December 14 to stockholders of record on November 30. There were 51,498 shares of this stock outstanding. On December 14, the company mailed dividend checks amounting to a total of $463,482 to stockholders.

REQUIRED

A. Journalize the dividend declaration of September 17.
B. Journalize the dividend payment of December 14.

3. Stanley H. Stern has been the single proprietor of an auto parts store. Below is shown his balance sheet as of September 30. On October 1, he admits Mr. John Q. Public as a 50% partner with the new company to be called Stern and Public. Under their partnership agreement, Mr. Public is to invest merchandise inventory valued at $49,576, store equipment valued at $15,000, and $44,184 in cash. The assets of Mr. Stern become the property of the partnership and his liabilities are assumed by Stern and Public.

S. H. STERN AUTO PARTS
Balance Sheet
As of September 30, 19____

ASSETS		LIABILITIES	
Cash	$35,596	Notes payable	$28,000
Accounts receivable .	41,180	Accounts payable . . .	24,000
Inventory	69,724	Taxes payable	1,040
Store equipment	15,300	Total liabilities	$ 53,040
Total assets	$161,800		
		OWNER'S EQUITY	
		S. H. Stern, capital	108,760
		Total liabilities and owner's equity	$161,800

REQUIRED

A. Assuming a new set of books is opened for the partnership, journalize and post the opening entries.

B. Prepare an opening day balance sheet for the partnership.

4. Marsha Frick and Susan Frack have been competitors in the wholesale drug business. On July 1 of the current year they form a partnership to be operated under the firm name of Frick and Frack. Their balance sheets as of June 30 are reproduced below. The partnership agreement provides that the assets are to be taken over at their book value and that the liabilities are to be as-

sumed by the partnership. The agreement also provides that Ms. Frack is to contribute a sufficient amount of additional cash to make her investment equal to Ms. Frick's investment. It is also agreed that the partners are to share profits and losses equally.

REQUIRED

Assuming that a new set of books is installed by the partnership, prepare the necessary opening entries in general journal form to record the investments of the partners.

MARSHA FRICK
Balance Sheet
June 30, 19___

ASSETS			LIABILITIES		
Cash		$ 8,250	Notes payable		$3,500
Accounts receivable	$6,732		Accounts payable		5,475
Less: Allowance for doubtful accounts	227		Social security tax payable		186
		6,505	Employees income tax payable		160
Merchandise inventory		10,279	**Total liabilities**		$ 9,321
Delivery equipment	$7,200				
Less: Accumulated depreciation	1,400				
		5,800	**OWNER'S EQUITY**		
Office equipment	$3,400		Marsha Frick, capital		23,913
Less: Accumulated depreciation	1,000		**Total liabilities and owner's equity**		$33,234
		2,400			
Total assets		$33,234			

SUSAN FRACK
Balance Sheet
June 30, 19___

ASSETS			LIABILITIES		
Cash		$10,680	Accounts payable		$9,925
Accounts receivable	$5,483		Social security tax payable		174
Less: Allowance for doubtful accounts	186		Employees income tax payable		158
		5,297	**Total liabilities**		$10,257
Merchandise inventory		8,721			
Delivery equipment	$7,400				
Less: Accumulated depreciation	1,800		**OWNER'S EQUITY**		
		5,600	Susan Frack, capital		22,641
Office equipment	$3,200		**Total liabilities and owner's equity**		$32,898
Less: Accumulated depreciation	600				
		2,600			
Total assets		$32,898			

CHAPTER 10

Tax Principles—
"There Are No Secrets,
Only Different Interpretations"

As the saying goes, "Nothing in life is sure, except death and a dreaded fear of April 15th."

As a consumer and/or business owner, you are subject to taxation and regulation by the federal, the state, and the local governments. Taxation requires you to keep records that you might not usually take the time to keep. Although some business authorities claim that the I.R.S. helps make marginal businesses successful because they are forced to keep adequate records, the "pressure" of state sales tax, FICA, withholding, tax deposits, worker's compensation, and federal income tax reporting requirements *forces* you to keep good records or fail at business. But there are other even more important reasons for your understanding state and federal tax regulations. They are:

a. The ability to institute business decisions based on taking advantage (legally, of course) of tax laws

b. The ability to make the investment and financial plans necessary to keep your earnings and your equity in your investments and personal finances

The tax laws and regulations are complicated and subject to yearly changes. To keep abreast of any changes and to maximize your understanding of tax planning and reporting, I recommend that you use an experienced accountant. *But,* you have to know about the tax laws to use an accountant's expertise most productively.

In this chapter, you'll learn about reporting and recording taxes, and tax planning. You will be able to handle all the basics involved with the tax collections you must make, the taxes you must pay, and the regulations you must comply with *before* you meet with an accountant. This will mean an immediate savings for you and/or your business, because you will be able to handle the preliminaries without the need (or cost) of an accountant.

TAXES: RECORDKEEPING AND RECORDING

Sales Taxes

Most states have *sales taxes*. The retailer (or wholesaler) that sells to the consumer collects these sales taxes, prepares a quarterly report, and remits the taxes collected to the state. Prior to opening his or her doors for business, a business owner must get a sales-tax number and the necessary forms from the state controller's office. A reporting form for the State of California is shown in Illustration 10.1.

ILLUSTRATION 10.1
California Sales and Use Tax Return

BT-401-AC3 FRONT REV. 11 (7-82)
STATE OF CALIFORNIA
BOARD OF EQUALIZATION – Department of Business Taxes

STATE, LOCAL and DISTRICT SALES and USE TAX RETURN

DUE ON OR BEFORE		FOR		PERIOD	YEAR

Mail to:

STATE BOARD OF EQUALIZATION

P. O. BOX 1799
SACRAMENTO, CA 95808

PARTIAL PERIOD

BUSINESS CODE	AREA CODE	ACCOUNT NUMBER

NAME

WORK COPY

BUSINESS ADDRESS

Not acceptable as a Return by the

CITY **State Board of Equalization** | REPORTING BASIS

READ INSTRUCTIONS BEFORE PREPARING

STATE SALES AND USE TAX

1. TOTAL (GROSS) SALES .... IF YOU INCLUDE TAX CHARGED – SEE LINE 9 ... $
2. ADD–Purchase price of tangible personal property purchased without California sales or use tax and used for some purpose other than resale ENTER "NONE" IF YOU HAVE NOTHING TO REPORT
3. TOTAL (Line 1 plus Line 2)   ENTER "NONE" IF YOU HAVE NOTHING TO REPORT ... $
   DEDUCT EXEMPT TRANSACTIONS (See Instructions)
4. Sales to other retailers for purposes of resale ... $
5. Nontaxable Sales of Food Products ......
6. Nontaxable Labor (Repair and Installation) ......
7. Sales to the United States Government ......
8. Sales in interstate or foreign commerce to out-of-state consumers .....
9. Amount of sales tax (if any) included in Line 1 .....
10. Other exempt transactions (See Instruction 10)
11. TOTAL TRANSACTIONS EXEMPT FROM STATE & COUNTY SALES & USE TAX (Lines 4 thru 10)..
12. Amount on which STATE & COUNTY Sales and Use Tax applies (Line 3 minus Line 11) ... $
13. AMOUNT OF TAX ...... 5% (4¾% State, ¼% County) (Multiply amount on Line 12 by .05) ...... $

UNIFORM LOCAL SALES AND USE TAX

14. Amount on which State Tax applies (Enter amount from Line 12) ... $
15. Adjustments (See Instruction 15) ...... $
16. Amount on which LOCAL Tax applies (Line 14 plus or minus Line 15) ... $
17. AMOUNT OF LOCAL TAX 1% (Multiply amount on Line 16 by .01) ...... $

DISTRICT SALES AND USE TAX

18a. Amount of San Francisco Bay Area Rapid Transit District Tax (From Line A12 Column A of Schedule A) ...... a $
18b. Amount of Santa Clara County Transit District Tax (From Line A12 Column B of Schedule A) ...... d $
18c. Amount of Santa Cruz Metropolitan Transit District Tax (From Line A12 Column C of Schedule A) ...... e $
18d. Amount of Los Angeles County Transportation Commission Tax (From Line A12 Column D of Schedule A) ...... f $
18e. Amount of San Mateo County Transit District Tax (From Line A12 Column E of Schedule A) ...... b $

TOTAL TAX

19. TOTAL STATE, COUNTY, LOCAL & DISTRICT TAX (Total of Lines 13, 17, 18a, b, c, d & e) **TOTAL TAX** $
20. Deduct amount of sales or use tax or reimbursement therefor imposed by other states and paid by you on the purchase of tangible personal property. Purchase price must be included in Line 2. (See Instructions 20)
21. NET STATE, COUNTY, LOCAL AND DISTRICT TAX (Line 19 minus Line 20) ...... $
22. LESS–Tax Prepayments | 1ST PAYMENT | 2ND PAYMENT | Total Prepayments
23. REMAINING STATE, COUNTY, LOCAL AND DISTRICT TAX (Line 21 minus Line 22) ...... $
24. Penalty of 10% (.10) if payment is made after the due date shown above ...... Penalty
25. Annual interest of 18% (.00049315 each day) is due if the payment is made after the above due date. Example: .00049315 × tax × number of days late = interest due ...... Interest
26. TOTAL AMOUNT DUE AND PAYABLE (Line 23 plus Lines 24 & 25) ...... $

I hereby certify that this return, including any accompanying schedules and statements, has been examined by me and to the best of my knowledge and belief is a true, correct and complete return.

SIGNATURE AND TITLE _____ ( )

MAKE CHECK OR MONEY ORDER PAYABLE TO STATE BOARD OF EQUALIZATION   PHONE NUMBER
Always Write Your Account Number on Your Check or Money Order

In your accounting records, you must record sales tax collected in a liability account called Sales Tax Collected in your General Ledger and/or Sales Journal. If sales are made on credit, the account receivable should be equal to the amount of sale plus the sales tax. In the following example, assume you are in California and the sales tax is 6%.

TRANSACTION

Mr. Smith buys a coat for $100 on account.

Accounts Receivable: Smith		Sales		Sales Tax Collected	
106			100		6
($100 sale + $6 tax)					

TRANSACTION

Mr. Smith pays the $106 he owes.

Accounts Receivable: Smith		Cash		Sales		Sales Tax Collected	
106	106	106			100		6
	(to record payment of sale + tax)	(to record receipt of payment)					

TRANSACTION

The sales tax is remitted to the state.

Cash		Sales		Sales Tax Collected	
106	6		100	6	6
	(to record remittance of tax)			(to record remittance of tax)	

If you are ever audited by the state, your accounting records plus your consecutively numbered sales receipts will provide adequate evidence of sales taxes collected.

Many small businesspeople become trapped because they fail to remember that the taxes collected must be remitted to the state. By comingling their cash with taxes collected, they overestimate their working cash and run into cash-flow problems. Don't let it happen to you!

Miscellaneous Taxes

A business is subject to other taxes, including:

a. Personal property taxes for equipment and inventory levied by cities, school districts, counties and states
b. Real property taxes for land and buildings
c. Excise taxes levied on specific commodities and products

Property taxes are imposed on property (real or personal) according to value (in Latin—ad valorem). The assessed value is generally recorded as a percentage of the *appraised value*. The methods of appraisal vary from state to state, but the appraisal is based upon how much money the taxing authority needs to raise. *The assesed value multiplied by the tax rate (%) equals the tax liability.* So, if you own property with a fair market value of $200,000 with an assessment rate of 80%, your assessed value is $160,000 (200,000 × .80). If the tax rate is 25%, your tax liability is $40,000 (160,000 × .25). Personal property taxes are figured in a similar fashion, and are levied on equipment and inventory.

Real estate and personal property taxes are business expenses. As such, they are entered on *Schedule C* of a *Form 1040 Income Tax return* for single proprietorships and a *Form 1120* for corporations. In your ledger, the amount of tax should be debited in the Property Tax Expense account and credited in the Property Tax Payable account.

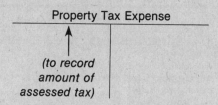

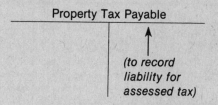

When the amount of the tax is remitted to the appropriate government, the Property Tax Payable account should be debited and the Cash account should be credited.

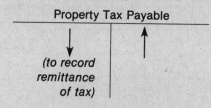

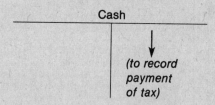

Excise taxes are levied on specific commodities, such as tobacco products, alcoholic beverages, automobiles, and gasoline. If you manufacture or sell items subject to federal excise tax, you must file a *Form 720* and make federal tax deposits. And, if you sell guns or alcohol you become subject to an *occupational tax*. Full information regarding excise taxes can be found in I.R.S. Publication 334, "Tax Guide for Small Business."

Federal Income Tax

The federal income tax laws are both complex and subject to frequent changes. Yet you as a businessperson and consumer need to understand these laws. This is because your knowledge of these laws has a direct bearing on your ability to generate business profits and maintain personal income.

Filing and Forms

Anyone above the poverty level must file a tax return. You may file a single, joint (married), or head of household return based upon your family and dependent (exemption) status. Individuals must file Form 1040 (Illustration 10.2) or the "short form" 1040A (Illustration 10.3). Form 1040 contains additional schedules for computing the data for various activities in which individuals and businesses engage. There are also special features of the tax laws requiring special treatment.

ILLUSTRATION 10.2
Form 1040

Form 1040 Department of the Treasury—Internal Revenue Service
U.S. Individual Income Tax Return 1982 (O)

For the year January 1–December 31, 1982, or other tax year beginning _____ 1982, ending _____ 19 _____ | OMB No. 1545-0074

Use IRS label. Otherwise, please print or type.

Your first name and initial (if joint return, also give spouse's name and initial) | Last name | **Your social security number**

Present home address (Number and street, including apartment number, or rural route) | **Spouse's social security no.**

City, town or post office, State and ZIP code | Your occupation ▶ | Spouse's occupation ▶

Presidential Election Campaign ▶ Do you want $1 to go to this fund? . . . . [ ] Yes [ ] No
If joint return, does your spouse want $1 to go to this fund? . . . [ ] Yes [ ] No

Note: *Checking "Yes" will not increase your tax or reduce your refund.*

For Privacy Act and Paperwork Reduction Act Notice, see Instructions.

Filing Status
Check only one box.

1 ____ Single
2 ____ Married filing joint return (even if only one had income)
3 ____ Married filing separate return. Enter spouse's social security no. above and full name here ▶ _____
4 ____ Head of household (with qualifying person). (See page 6 of Instructions.) If the qualifying person is your unmarried child but not your dependent, enter child's name ▶ _____
5 ____ Qualifying widow(er) with dependent child (Year spouse died ▶ 19 ____). (See page 6 of Instructions.)

Exemptions
Always check the box labeled Yourself. Check other boxes if they apply.

6a ____ Yourself   ____ 65 or over   ____ Blind } Enter number of boxes checked on 6a and b ▶ ____
 b ____ Spouse   ____ 65 or over   ____ Blind }
 c First names of your dependent children who lived with you ▶ _____ } Enter number of children listed on 6c ▶ ____

d Other dependents: (1) Name	(2) Relationship	(3) Number of months lived in your home	(4) Did dependent have income of $1,000 or more?	(5) Did you provide more than one-half of dependent's support?

Enter number of other dependents ▶ ____
Add numbers entered in boxes above ▶ ____

e Total number of exemptions claimed . . . .

Income
Please attach Copy B of your Forms W–2 here.
If you do not have a W–2, see page 5 of Instructions.

7 Wages, salaries, tips, etc.	7	
8 Interest income *(attach Schedule B if over $400 or you have any All-Savers interest)*	8	
9a Dividends *(attach Schedule B if over $400)* _____ , 9b Exclusion _____		
c Subtract line 9b from line 9a	9c	
10 Refunds of State and local income taxes *(do not enter an amount unless you deducted those taxes in an earlier year—see page 9 of Instructions)*	10	
11 Alimony received	11	
12 Business income or (loss) *(attach Schedule C)* . . . . ▶	12	
13 Capital gain or (loss) *(attach Schedule D)*	13	
14 40% capital gain distributions not reported on line 13 (See page 9 of Instructions)	14	
15 Supplemental gains or (losses) *(attach Form 4797)*	15	
16 Fully taxable pensions, IRA distributions, and annuities not reported on line 17 . .	16	
17a Other pensions and annuities. Total received 17a		
b Taxable amount, if any, from worksheet on page 10 of Instructions	17b	
18 Rents, royalties, partnerships, estates, trusts, etc. *(attach Schedule E)*	18	
19 Farm income or (loss) *(attach Schedule F)* . . . . ▶	19	
20a Unemployment compensation (insurance). Total received 20a		
b Taxable amount, if any, from worksheet on page 10 of Instructions	20b	
21 Other income (state nature and source—see page 10 of Instructions) ▶ _____	21	
22 **Total income.** Add amounts in column for lines 7 through 21 . . . . ▶	22	

Please attach check or money order here.

Adjustments to Income
(See Instructions on page 11)

23 Moving expense *(attach Form 3903 or 3903F)* . . .	23	
24 Employee business expenses *(attach Form 2106)* . .	24	
25 Payments to an IRA. You **must** enter code from page 11 (_____)	25	
26 Payments to a Keogh *(H.R. 10)* retirement plan . . .	26	
27 Penalty on early withdrawal of savings	27	
28 Alimony paid	28	
29 Deduction for a married couple when both work *(attach Schedule W)*	29	
30 Disability income exclusion *(attach Form 2440)* . .	30	
31 **Total adjustments.** Add lines 23 through 30 . . . . ▶		31

Adjusted Gross Income

32 **Adjusted gross income.** Subtract line 31 from line 22. If this line is less than $10,000, see "Earned Income Credit" (line 62) on page 15 of Instructions. If you want IRS to figure your tax, see page 3 of Instructions . . . . ▶ | 32 |

✩U.S. GOVERNMENT PRINTING OFFICE 1982 363–300

E I #52-1074467

Form 1040 (1982)   Page **2**

Tax Compu- tation (See Instruc- tions on page 12)	33 Amount from line 32 *(adjusted gross income)*	33
	34a If you itemize, complete Schedule A (Form 1040) and enter the amount from Schedule A, line 30	34a
	Caution: If you have unearned income and can be claimed as a dependent on your parent's return, check here ▶ ☐ and see page 12 of the Instructions. Also see page 12 of the Instructions if: ● *You are married filing a separate return and your spouse itemizes deductions, OR* ● *You file Form 4563, OR* ● *You are a dual-status alien.*	
	34b If you do not itemize, complete the worksheet on page 13. Then enter the allowable part of your charitable contributions here	34b
	35 Subtract line 34a or 34b, whichever applies, from line 33	35
	36 Multiply $1,000 by the total number of exemptions claimed on Form 1040, line 6e . .	36
	37 Taxable Income. Subtract line 36 from line 35	37
	38 Tax. Enter tax here and check if from ☐ Tax Table, ☐ Tax Rate Schedule X, Y, or Z, or ☐ Schedule G	38
	39 Additional Taxes. (See page 13 of Instructions.) Enter here and check if from ☐ Form 4970,⎫ ☐ Form 4972, ☐ Form 5544, or ☐ section 72 penalty taxes . . . . ⎭	39
	40 **Total.** Add lines 38 and 39 . . . . ▶	40

Credits (See Instruc- tions on page 13)	41 Credit for the elderly *(attach Schedules R&RP)*	41	
	42 Foreign tax credit *(attach Form 1116)*	42	
	43 Investment credit *(attach Form 3468)*	43	
	44 Partial credit for political contributions	44	
	45 Credit for child and dependent care expenses (*attach* *Form 2441*).	45	
	46 Jobs credit *(attach Form 5884)*	46	
	47 Residential energy credit *(attach Form 5695)*	47	
	48 Other credits—see page 14 ▶	48	
	49 **Total credits.** Add lines 41 through 48	49	
	50 **Balance.** Subtract line 49 from line 40 and enter difference (but not less than zero) . ▶	50	

Other Taxes (Including Advance EIC Payments)	51 Self-employment tax *(attach Schedule SE)*	51
	52 Minimum tax *(attach Form 4625)*	52
	53 Alternative minimum tax *(attach Form 6251)*	53
	54 Tax from recapture of investment credit *(attach Form 4255)*	54
	55 Social security (FICA) tax on tip income not reported to employer *(attach Form 4137)* .	55
	56 Uncollected employee FICA and RRTA tax on tips *(from Form W–2)*	56
	57 Tax on an IRA *(attach Form 5329)*	57
	58 Advance earned income credit (EIC) payments received *(from Form W–2)*	58
06	59 **Total tax.** Add lines 50 through 58 . . . . ■	59

Payments Attach Forms W–2, W–2G, and W–2P to front.	60 Total Federal income tax withheld	60	
	61 1982 estimated tax payments and amount applied from 1981 return .	61	
	62 Earned income credit. If line 33 is under $10,000, see page 15 of Instructions	62	
	63 Amount paid with Form 4868	63	
	64 Excess FICA and RRTA tax withheld (two or more employers) .	64	
	65 Credit for Federal tax on special fuels and oils *(attach Form 4136)*	65	
	66 Regulated Investment Company credit *(attach Form 2439)*	66	
	67 **Total.** Add lines 60 through 66 . . . . ▶	67	

Refund or Amount You Owe	68 If line 67 is larger than line 59, enter amount **OVERPAID** . . . . ▶	68
	69 Amount of line 68 to be **REFUNDED TO YOU** . . . . ▶	69
	70 Amount of line 68 to be applied to your 1983 estimated tax . . . ▶	70	
	71 If line 59 is larger than line 67, enter **AMOUNT YOU OWE.** Attach check or money order for full amount payable to Internal Revenue Service. Write your social security number and "1982 Form 1040" on it. ▶	71
	*(Check ▶ ☐ if Form 2210 (2210F) is attached. See page 16 of Instructions.) ▶ $	

Please Sign Here	Under penalties of perjury, I declare that I have examined this return, including accompanying schedules and statements, and to the best of my knowledge and belief, it is true, correct, and complete. Declaration of preparer (other than taxpayer) is based on all information of which preparer has any knowledge.
	▶ _____ | _____ ▶ _____ Your signature Date Spouse's signature (if filing jointly, BOTH must sign)

Paid Preparer's Use Only	Preparer's ▶ signature	Date	Check if self-em- ployed ▶ ☐	Preparer's social security no.
	Firm's name (or yours, if self-employed) ▶ and address		E.I. No. ▶ ZIP code ▶	

ILLUSTRATION 10.3
Form 1040A

1982 Department of the Treasury — Internal Revenue Service
Form 1040A US Individual Income Tax Return (0)   OMB No. 1545-0085

Step 1
Name and address
Use the IRS mailing label. Otherwise, print or type.

Your first name and initial (if joint return, also give spouse's name and initial)   Last name   Your social security no.

Present home address   Spouse's social security no.

City, town or post office, State, and ZIP code   Your occupation
Spouse's occupation

Presidential Election Campaign Fund
Do you want $1 to go to this fund?. . . . . ☐ Yes   ☐ No
If joint return, does your spouse want $1 to go to this fund? ☐ Yes   ☐ No

Step 2
Filing status
(Check only one)
and Exemptions

1 ☐ Single (See if you can use Form 1040EZ.)
2 ☐ Married filing joint return (even if only one had income)
3 ☐ Married filing separate return. Enter spouse's social security no. above and full name here. _____
4 ☐ Head of household (with qualifying person). If the qualifying person is your unmarried child but not your dependent, write this child's name here. _____

Always check the exemption box labeled Yourself. Check other boxes if they apply.

5a ☐ Yourself   ☐ 65 or over   ☐ Blind   Write number of boxes checked on 5a and b ☐
 b ☐ Spouse   ☐ 65 or over   ☐ Blind
 c First names of your dependent children who lived with you _____ Write number of children listed on 5c ☐

Attach Copy B of Forms W-2 here

d Other dependents: (1) Name	(2) Relationship	(3) Number of months lived in your home.	(4) Did dependent have income of $1,000 or more?	(5) Did you provide more than one-half of dependent's support?

Write number of other dependents listed on 5d ☐

e Total number of exemptions claimed . . . .   Add numbers entered in boxes above ☐

Step 3
Adjusted gross income

6 Wages, salaries, tips, etc. *(Attach Forms W-2)*. . . . . 6 _____
7 Interest income *(Complete page 2 if over $400 or you have any All-Savers interest)*. . . . . . 7 _____
8a Dividends _____ (Complete page 2 if over $400) 8b Exclusion _____ Subtract line 8b from 8a . . 8c _____
9a Unemployment compensation (insurance). Total from Form(s) 1099-UC _____
 b Taxable amount, if any, from worksheet on page 16 of Instructions. . . . . 9b _____
10 Add lines 6, 7, 8c, and 9b. This is your total income. . . . . 10 _____
11 Deduction for a married couple when both work. Complete the worksheet on page 17. . . . . . 11 _____
12 Subtract line 11 from line 10. This is your adjusted gross income. . . . . 12 _____

Step 4
Taxable income

13 Allowable part of your charitable contributions. Complete the worksheet on page 18. . . . . . 13 _____
14 Subtract line 13 from line 12. . . . . 14 _____
15 Multiply $1,000 by the total number of exemptions claimed in box 5e. . . . . 15 _____
16 Subtract line 15 from line 14. This is your taxable income. . . . . 16 _____

Step 5
Tax, credits, and payments
Attach check or money order here

17a Partial credit for political contributions. See page 19. . . . . . . ■ 17a _____
  b Total Federal income tax withheld, from W-2 form(s). *(If line 6 is more than $32,400, see page 19.)*. . . . . 17b _____
     Stop Here and Sign Below If You Want IRS to Figure Your Tax
  c Earned income credit, from worksheet on page 21. . . . . 17c _____
18 Add lines 17a, b, and c. These are your total credits and payments. . . . . 18 _____
19a Find tax on amount on line 16. Use tax table, pages 26-31. . . . . . 19a _____
  b Advance EIC payment *(from W-2 form(s))*. . . . . 19b _____
20 Add lines 19a and 19b. This is your total tax. . . . . 20 _____

Step 6
Refund or amount you owe

21 If line 18 is larger than line 20, subtract line 20 from line 18. Enter the amount to be **refunded to you**. . . . . 21 _____
22 If line 20 is larger than line 18, subtract line 18 from line 20. Enter the **amount you owe.** Attach payment for full amount payable to "Internal Revenue Service.". . . . . 22 _____

Step 7
Sign your return

I have read this return and any attachments filed with it. Under penalties of perjury, I declare that to the best of my knowledge and belief, the return and attachments are correct and complete.

Your signature   Date   ▶   Spouse's signature (If filing jointly, BOTH must sign)

Paid preparer's signature   Date   Check if self-employed ☐   Preparer's social security no.

Firm's name (or yours, if self-employed) _____
Address and Zip code   E.I. no. _____

For **Privacy Act and Paperwork Reduction Act Notice,** see page 34.

Following is a list of schedules for Form 1040 (file only the ones needed as a result of your taxable activities):

Schedule A—Itemized Deductions
Schedule B—Dividend and Interest Income
Schedule C—Profit (or loss) from Business or Profession
Schedule D—Capital Gains and Losses
Schedule E—Supplemental Income
Schedule G—Income Averaging
Schedule R—Retirement Income Credit Computation
Schedule TC—For Adjusted Gross Income Over $20,000 ($40,000 for married couples)

Schedule C of Form 1040 is the one used to report business operations for single proprietorships. Partnerships file a *Form 1065*, but each partner must file a Form 1040 for the income taken from the partnership. A corporation files a *Form 1120*. A Subchapter S corporation files a *Form 1120-S* (Informational Report). Owners of a corporation must file a Form 1040, as in a partnership.

Proprietors and partners *must* pay estimated income tax quarterly, since they are not included in payroll withholding. They have to file a *Form 1040 ES* (Illustration 10.4) for the current year on or before April 15. This form is generally submitted with the Form 1040 from the previous year. One-fourth of the estimated tax liability for the current year (based on estimated income and exemptions) is remitted with the 1040 ES; like amounts should be remitted prior to June 15, September 15, and January 15.

ILLUSTRATION 10.4
Form 1040 ES

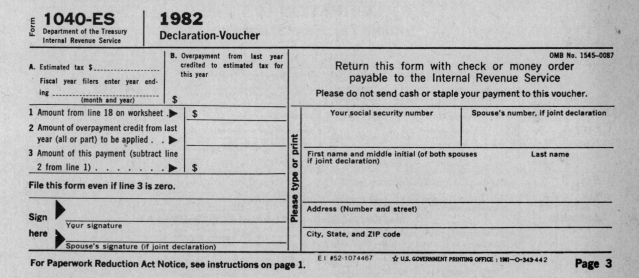

The Basic Tax Formula

The basic tax formula for computing your tax for an individual return on the Form 1040 is:

1. Gross Income = Total Income − Exclusions
2. Adjusted Gross Income (AGI) = Gross Income − Deductions
3. Taxable Income = Adjusted Gross Income − Deductions − Exemptions
4. Gross Tax Liability = Taxable Income × Tax Rates
5. Net Tax Payable = Gross Tax Liability − Tax Credits − Prepayments

The *total income* part of the formula includes:

a. Wages and salary, interest, and stock dividends (from Schedule B)

b. Rents, royalties, pensions, or profits from a partnership or Subchapter S corporation (from Schedule E)

c. Income (or loss) from a single proprietorship (from Schedule C)

The results from these schedules are entered on the Form 1040 and you arrive at *adjusted gross income* (AGI).

Income earned in a trade or business from selling goods or services is taxed at ordinary income tax rates. However, income earned from the sale of an asset (i.e., land, equipment), which was held for longer than the required holding period, now twelve months, is considered a *long-term capital gain*. A long-term capital gain and capital gains deductions are first entered on Schedule D; the result is then entered on the Form 1040.

Once you have determined your adjusted gross income, your next step is to subtract *deductions*, the so-called *Standard Deduction*, which was $3,200 in 1981, or *Itemized Deductions* from Schedule A. Itemized deductions from AGI include:

a. Medical—Part (%) of medical insurance premiums, drugs, medicine, doctors' fees, nurses, hospital fees, dental bills, etc.

b. Taxes—real estate tax on your home, state and local income tax, gas, sales tax, and personal property tax.

c. Interest Expense—loans, credit cards, mortgages

d. Contributions—charities, religious, and other eligible causes

ILLUSTRATION 10.5
Income Tax Rate Schedule

1982 Tax Rate Schedules   Your zero bracket amount has been built into these Tax Rate Schedules.

Caution: You must use the Tax Table instead of these Tax Rate Schedules if your taxable income is less than $50,000 unless you use Schedule G (income averaging), to figure your tax. In that case, even if your taxable income is less than $50,000, use the rate schedules on this page to figure your tax.

Schedule X

Single Taxpayers
Use this Schedule if you checked Filing Status Box 1 on Form 1040—

If the amount on Form 1040, line 37 is: Over—	But not Over—	Enter on Form 1040, line 38	of the amount over—
$0	$2,300	—0—	
2,300	3,400	............12%	$2,300
3,400	4,400	$132+14%	3,400
4,400	6,500	272+16%	4,400
6,500	8,500	608+17%	6,500
8,500	10,800	948+19%	8,500
10,800	12,900	1,385+22%	10,800
12,900	15,000	1,847+23%	12,900
15,000	18,200	2,330+27%	15,000
18,200	23,500	3,194+31%	18,200
23,500	28,800	4,837+35%	23,500
28,800	34,100	6,692+40%	28,800
34,100	41,500	8,812+44%	34,100
41,500	....	12,068+50%	41,500

Schedule Z

Unmarried Heads of Household
(including certain married persons who live apart (and abandoned spouses)—see page 6 of the instructions)
Use this schedule if you checked Filing Status Box 4 on Form 1040—

If the amount on Form 1040, line 37 is: Over—	But not Over—	Enter on Form 1040, line 38	of the amount over—
$0	$2,300	—0—	
2,300	4,400	............12%	$2,300
4,400	6,500	$252+14%	4,400
6,500	8,700	546+16%	6,500
8,700	11,800	898+20%	8,700
11,800	15,000	1,518+22%	11,800
15,000	18,200	2,222+23%	15,000
18,200	23,500	2,958+28%	18,200
23,500	28,800	4,442+32%	23,500
28,800	34,100	6,138+38%	28,800
34,100	44,700	8,152+41%	34,100
44,700	60,600	12,498+49%	44,700
60,600	....	20,289+50%	60,600

Schedule Y
Married Taxpayers and Qualifying Widows and Widowers

Married Filing Joint Returns and Qualifying Widows and Widowers
Use this schedule if you checked Filing Status Box 2 or 5 on Form 1040—

If the amount on Form 1040, line 37 is: Over—	But not Over—	Enter on Form 1040, line 38	of the amount over—
$0	$3,400	—0—	
3,400	5,500	............12%	$3,400
5,500	7,600	$252+14%	5,500
7,600	11,900	546+16%	7,600
11,900	16,000	1,234+19%	11,900
16,000	20,200	2,013+22%	16,000
20,200	24,600	2,937+25%	20,200
24,600	29,900	4,037+29%	24,600
29,900	35,200	5,574+33%	29,900
35,200	45,800	7,323+39%	35,200
45,800	60,000	11,457+44%	45,800
60,000	85,600	17,705+49%	60,000
85,600	....	30,249+50%	85,600

Married Filing Separate Returns
Use this schedule if you checked Filing Status Box 3 on Form 1040—

If the amount on Form 1040, line 37 is: Over—	But not Over—	Enter on Form 1040, line 38	of the amount over—
$0	$1,700	—0—	
1,700	2,750	............12%	$1,700
2,750	3,800	$126.00+14%	2,750
3,800	5,950	273.00+16%	3,800
5,950	8,000	617.00+19%	5,950
8,000	10,100	1,006.50+22%	8,000
10,100	12,300	1,468.50+25%	10,100
12,300	14,950	2,018.50+29%	12,300
14,950	17,600	2,787.00+33%	14,950
17,600	22,900	3,651.50+39%	17,600
22,900	30,000	5,728.50+44%	22,900
30,000	42,800	8,852.50+49%	30,000
42,800	....	15,124.50+50%	42,800

e. Casualty and Theft Losses—personal or business

f. Miscellaneous—alimony paid, union dues, child care, cost of preparing tax return, investment expenses, etc.

To figure out your *taxable income*, you must subtract your exemptions from AGI. As of 1981, you were allowed a $1,000 exemption for yourself, spouse, and each dependent child. If you or your spouse is over 65, or if either of you is blind, you're entitled to additional exemptions. So, after you subtract your deductions and exemptions, you are left with taxable income.

To arrive at your *gross tax liability*, you need to use the appropriate tax schedule (Illustration 10.5) for your marital category. If you are single, you use *Schedule X*. If you are married, you use *Schedule Y*. If you are single but the head of the household, you use *Schedule Z*. Schedule TC must be used if:

1. As a single taxpayer your AGI is over $20,000
2. If married, your income is over $40,000

3. If you use Schedule G to income average

You'll notice when examining the schedule in Illustration 10.5 that the tax rates are *graduated*. The tax rate (%) increases as your AGI increases.

At this point, you can probably see that our tax laws are complex but, at the same time, you should also have a better understanding of how to arrive at the bottom line of the Form 1040 tax return. When you've computed your gross tax liability, you simply subtract any *tax credits* or *prepayments* to arrive at the *net tax payable*. The prepayments are derived from any money you remitted with the Form 1040 ES on your estimated tax liability. The tax credits are special deductions from your gross tax liability, which include work incentive (WIN), investment credit, foreign taxes, contributions to political candidates, and energy credits. Since these credits are deducted directly from your tax liability, they have an impact of several times that of a business expense on your tax bill. This is because they occur after the tax rates have been exercised.

Federal Income Tax Planning

Simply put, the basis for what you earn in your own business is the money you take in, minus any cost of goods sold, minus your operating expenses and finally, minus your income tax liability. You can (and should) increase your profits by getting better gross margins on cost of goods sold or by cutting expenses. But, even though you increase your net income, you don't get to keep all of it, because as your income goes up, the amount your Uncle Sam gets goes up, too. If you understand the tax laws and take all the deductions, allowances, and credits available to

you, you can reduce your tax liability and increase the amount of money you really keep after paying taxes.

You can increase what you keep through income tax planning and management. Hopefully, the prior sections of this chapter have helped to unravel some of the "mysteries" involved in the general mechanics of income tax reporting. The final part of this chapter has been set aside to explain some of the more complicated, but readily available ways to reduce your income tax liability.

Depreciation

The I.R.S. Code, Section 167 (f), permits you to neglect any *salvage value* when depreciating an asset with a life of three or more years. Therefore, you can depreciate the entire cost of the asset and still recover the salvage value when the asset is sold.

You can take a bonus depreciation of 20% the first year on assets with a useful life of six or more years and depreciate the balance by any I.R.S.-approved method. This is only useful for a business whose profits are high in the year the asset (i.e., truck) is purchased.

Investment Credit

When this credit is in effect, the tax laws allow you to deduct a certain percentage of the value of any tangible personal property for the year the property was purchased. You'll have to check current tax laws to see if this investment credit is in effect. It is a method the government uses to encourage consumers to invest their savings.

The investment credit applies directly to your tax bill. For example, a 10% investment credit would save you much more tax outlay than a 10% depreciation expense, which is subtracted from AGI.

Additional Ways to Minimize Tax Liability

A businessperson can reduce and thereby minimize his or her tax liability by taking the maximum expense deductions allowable under the tax laws. You should record and take all possible expense deductions for everything business related. You can also make high-expense purchases and use the deductions in anticipated high-profit years. For example, you can stock up on office supplies, pay rent in advance, and pre-pay expense bills which could be deferred until next year. You should review your memberships in associations and clubs, magazine subscriptions, automobile expenses, trips, education, interest paid, and other expenditures that you pay with personal funds to see if they legally constitute a business expense.

Where to Get Additional Information and Tax Assistance

There is a great deal of free information available from the I.R.S. on tax-return preparation. Just call or write your local I.R.S. office for the following publications:

a. "Your Federal Income Tax Return—For Individuals," I.R.S. Publication 17
b. "Tax Guide for Small Business," I.R.S. Publication 334

In addition, the I.R.S. will furnish you with detailed information on a large number of specific subjects. These should be obtained as the need arises.

After reading this chapter, you may ask yourself, "Do I dare try it on my own?" If you've prepared an individual return in the past, then adding a business of your own shouldn't pose any great problem. However (there usually is a "however") because you might miss some available deductions, you probably should consult an accountant *after* you've done the initial preparations. I do recommend some professional help at the onset of a new business. This help should follow the use of your knowledge in tax matters.

Don't be a chicken! Give it the old college try!

EXERCISES AND PROBLEMS
FOR CHAPTER 10

Tax Principles

Exercises

1. Ken Corre, M.D., files his income tax return on a cash basis. During the current year, he received $72,600 from patients for services given, and billed patients for an additional $69,500 for services given. At the end of the year, his accounts receivable of $21,500 related to this year's billings. What should Dr. Corre report as his gross income for the current year?

2. The following information relates to the income tax situation of John Ross for the current year:

Total income $108,000
Personal exemptions.......... 9,000
Deductions to determine AGI ... 7,650
Itemized deductions 11,840
Exclusions from gross income ... 2,120

REQUIRED

Determine the amount of the taxpayer's adjusted gross income (AGI) and the taxable income for the year. Assume the maximum limit for the standard deduction is $3,200.

Problems

1. Consider the income tax status of each of the items listed below. For each item, decide whether it should be "included in gross income" or "excluded from gross income" for federal income tax for individuals.

   a. Cash dividends received on stock.
   b. Gain on sale of an original oil painting.
   c. Interest received on New York City Bonds.
   d. Tips received by a waitress.
   e. Value of treasury bonds received as a gift.
   f. Salary received by principal stockholder of a corporation.
   g. A $1,000 note cancelled by the rendering of a service.
   h. A Las Vegas vacation was given as a reward for outstanding service.
   i. Share of income from partnership in excess of drawing.

2. Consider the deductibility status of each of the items listed below. State whether the item is "deducted to reach AGI," "deducted from AGI," or "not deductible."

   a. Cost of commuting between home and office.
   b. State sales tax paid for purchase of boat.
   c. Interest paid on personal debts.
   d. Capital loss on sale of stock.
   e. Fee paid to lawyer for advice.
   f. Travel expenses incurred by sales personnel (not reimbursed).
   g. Expenses incurred in moving to accept new job (not reimbursed).
   h. Damage to house caused by hurricane.

Solutions to Accounting Exercises and Problems

CHAPTERS 2-3

The Accounting Equation and Financial Statements

Exercises

1. $187,000.

2. $44,800.

3. Transaction		Total Assets	Total Liabilities	Total Owner's Equity
a.		+	+	NC
b.		+	NC	+
c.	(+ −)	NC	NC	NC
d.	(+ −)	NC	NC	NC
e.		—	NC	—
f.		—	—	NC
g.		—	—	NC

Problems

1A. XYZ Company

2A. Net Income = $1,917.07
  B. Assets $\quad$ = Liabilities + Owner's Equity
  $11,662.55 = $3,395.24 + $8,267.31

3B. Assets $\quad$ = Liabilities + Owner's Equity
  $25,579.50 = $1,620 $\quad$ + $23,959.50

4B. Net Income = $4,140.
  Assets $\quad$ = Liabilities + Owner's Equity
  $27,740 $\quad$ = $61,800 $\quad$ + $20,940

CHAPTER 4

Recordkeeping

Problems

1D. Net Income = $2,941.88
Assets   = Liabilities + Owner's Equity
$4,905.36 = $591.45 + $4,313.81

2D. Net Income = $3,266
Assets   = Liabilities + Owner's Equity

$128,264   = $24,078 + $104,186

3D. Net Income = $1,923
Assets   = Liabilities + Owner's Equity
$33,223   = $15,975 + $17,248

CHAPTER 5

The Desired Income Approach

Problems

1. *Revenue:*

Sales	$250,000
Cost of Goods Sold	150,000
Gross Profit (40%)	100,000
Expenses	75,000
Net Income	$ 25,000

3. *Revenue:*

Sales	$200,000
Cost of Goods Sold	

Beginning Inventory	1,923
+ Purchases During Year . .	100,000
Goods Available for Sale . .	101,923
− Ending Inventory	1,923
Cost of Goods Sold	100,000
Gross Profit	100,000
Operating Expenses	50,000
Expenses:	
Net Income	50,000

CHAPTER 6

Accounting for Cash

Exercises

1. $9,604

2A. No
B. Two people should handle complementary
accounting records.

Problems

1A. $14,070.34 = $14,070.34

3D. Net Income = $3,478.00
Assets   = Liabilities + Owner's Equity
$6,580.00 = $180.00   + $6,400.00

4C. Net Loss   = $400 $149,650.00 = $69,080.00 + $80,570.00
Assets   = Liabilities   + Owner's Equity

CHAPTER 7

Accrual Accounting

Exercises

1A. $20,000; $24,000
   B. 9.09%; 8%
   C. $72,000; 80%

2. $348,500.

Problems

1A. Net Income = $128,230
Assets   = Liabilities   + Owner's Equity
$240,026   = $34,300   + $205,726

2B. Net Income = $60,704
Assets   = Liabilities   + Owner's Equity
$402,176   = $93,472   + $308,704

3B. Net Income = $133,972.00
Assets   = Liabilities   + Owner's Equity
$387,566.00 = $179,968.00 + $207,598.00

4B. Net Loss   = [47620]
Assets   = Liabilities   + Owner's Equity
$129,630.00 = $39,900.00   + $89,730.00

CHAPTER 8

Payroll

Exercises

1C. $29,480.

Problems

1A. ———
   B. 160 hours @ $3.60 + 21 hours @ $5.40 (overtime rate).
   C. Wayne has more deductions (exemptions). This increases his monthly gross pay.

CHAPTER 9

Partnerships and Corporation

Exercises

1A. Smith gets $24,000. Jones gets $36,000.
  B. Smith gets $30,000. Jones gets $30,000.
  C. Smith gets $28,400. Jones gets $31,600.
  D. Smith gets $31,500. Jones gets $28,500.

Problems

1B. Net Income = $54,000. Frack gets $27,526.
                         Frick gets $26,474.
  C. Assets   = Liabilities + Owner's Equity
     $193,920 = $51,000 + $142,920

CHAPTER 10

Tax Principles

Exercises

1. $72,600 (cash received only).

2. $91,350.

  G. included
  H. included
  I. included

2A. not deductible
  B. deducted from A.G.I.
  C. deducted from A.G.I.
  D. deducted to reach A.G.I.
  E. deducted to reach A.G.I.
  F. deducted to reach A.G.I.
  G. deducted to reach A.G.I.
  H. deducted from A.G.I.

Problems

1A. included
  B. included
  C. excluded
  D. included
  E. excluded
  F. included

Index